Connecting The Dots

Thoughts from the Diary
of a Politically Incorrect
Mutual Fund Aficionado

Joseph Hardgrove

2nd Tier Publishing

Published by:
  2nd Tier Publishing
  501 Wimberley Oaks Dr
  Wimberley, TX 78676

ISBN 978-0-9894642-0-8

Book design by Dan Gauthier

Contents

About the Author

Joseph Hardgrove, a graduate of Texas A&M University is a former English teacher and technical writer/editor. He played basketball and baseball at Texas A&M and earned all Southwest Conference honors in 1955. He was a student assistant basketball coach at A&M and after graduation played professional baseball in the New York Giant Organization. He has been in the investment advisory business for more than 50 years.

Mr. Hardgrove has been a member of the American Funds Advisory Council since 1987 and is a registered investment advisor with Omega Wealth Partners Inc. He handled the direct sales organization of a major national medical association retirement plan utilizing mutual funds for more than 20 years.

A former Top of the Table, Million Dollar Round Table member, he is now retired from his Broker Dealer, Omega Securities Inc. and is CEO of the Omega Foundation Inc., a donor advised 501C3 charitable organization.

Mr. Hardgrove authors an investment newsletter entitled *Opinions & Facts*, which at its peak had a circulation of over 5,000. He is author of three other books: an isometric exercise publication, called *Trim Control*, a compilation of Christmas Eve short stories entitled, *Birds of a Feather* and a memoir, *When September Comes*.

To the Reader
A Personal Note

Please be advised that the articles and columns appearing in this book represent the writer's own opinion based on personal research relating to the accuracy and philosophy of the particular subject.

None of the articles were edited by any governmental organization or approved by any self regulatory group. The material from this book was drawn from a series of internal newsletters/articles and opinions designed primarily for clients of Omega Securities Inc. and Omega Wealth Partners Inc. exclusively. In addition there are certain reproduced letters and comments which express historical events and philosophies that applied during the time period that this book covers. You will also find a section of opinion editorials which represents the separate thoughts of the author that were included in *Opinions & Facts* over a period of years.

We hope to alert and remind readers about positive and negative actions taken by governments and business entities in the very short time period covered in this book. The opinions expressed here certainly represent that of the author, based on 50 years' experience in the financial advisory business.

It goes without saying, that there is no guarantee future investments described will yield the same results as in the past. And there is no guarantee of positive return on the investments. Any investment the reader makes should be done only after reading the prospectus and discussing possibilities with an experienced investment advisor.

An Additional Note

This book is not written in chapters.

Section I covers various articles from *Opinions & Facts* that I've included. Regarding events that have occurred over the timeline shown, you will notice that I've not described connective time periods that I have shown random years with comments.

Section II represents letters and articles that we have written to our clients. Many are on a personal basis and most of the comments reflect encouraging and positive ideas.

Section III is made up strictly of "opinions"—these were basic editorials that we wrote at the end of many of our *Opinions & Facts* articles. We've commented on, not only investment ideas but cultural and meaningful governmental changes that have occurred over the period.

It is my suggestion that as you read the book, you will see very little linkage between the sections; however, as you read it you will note we have attempted to make the headlines of interest. This makes it possible for you, the reader, to be able to go over the book at any time, and read our thoughts without being linked up with chapters written earlier.

I hope this book is not only educational but also entertaining and will give you a different and often times controversial take on financials and events that happened over the last several years. We hope that it will give both the investor and investment advisor a view of the past which should benefit them in the future.

We agree with the statement that Mark Twain reportedly made regarding history: "History does not necessarily repeat itself—but it rhymes."

We hope that this book is not only educational but also entertaining and will give you a different and oftentimes controversial take on everyday financials.

Please note that much of the information discussed in this book was gleaned from various sources. Among these publications were The Wall Street Journal; Barron's; the New York Times; The Fort Worth Star Telegram; The Dallas Morning News; Newsweek; Nick Murray's Monthly Newsletter†; Business Week and Fox News; U S News and World report; USA Today; Los Angeles Times; the Economists; and Opinions & Facts.

† Nick Murray is the author of 11 books for financial services. For more information go to www.nickmurray.com

Forward

This book is written in an attempt to give the reader a picture of mid 20th Century investing concepts during a half century of differing economic and cultural changes.

While it is not intended to be autobiographical, in a few cases we refer to personal relationships, obligations and experiences to give the reader an economic and investment timeline of the last several decades.

Most of the items come from our publication *Opinions & Facts*. This document was designed to be a periodic "Information Letter" as opposed to a "Newsletter."

We have commented on news that has been generated over this period of time. We hope that we've provided information to clients, and associated industry persons, regarding investing, insurance, inflation, politics, cultural phenomena, and various other elements which affect an individual's financial life. We have also projected ideas and opinions about governments, companies and real life experiences as we observed them.

Please know that each article or column represents our own opinion in addressing financial activities. One of the main reasons for writing this account is to alert and remind us all how both governments and businesses forget too soon the errors made just a few summers ago while ignoring economic truths that have existed for generations.

The reader must be alerted that if he seeks a liberal or progressive slant to the economics in this document, he'll be hard pressed to find them. The philosophy that is expressed here represents that of the author based on more than 50 years of study and experience in the financial advisory field.

There is no guarantee that the future will yield the same positive results as in the past.

We welcome you to a look-back over our first fifty years of a most challenging, varied, eventful and exciting career that individuals and a company could possibly experience. During this period, I, my associates, and countless thousands of friends from all over the world have enjoyed sharing and listening to stories of sad and tragic times, as well as glowing sunny days which gave us hope for the future.

This is the way equity markets work, and incidentally, it's the way real life works.

Section I

Selected Articles

From *Opinions & Facts*

A Periodic Publication of

Omega Securities, Inc.

1992
Observation – Current

July of 1992; this was a time when we had what we thought to be a "runaway" national debt, but it wasn't near what it has become in the 21st century.

In recent years the movement to a global economy has provided higher wages to more highly skilled and educated individuals at the upper income levels, while the wages of moderately skilled workers at middle and lower income levels have stayed level or decreased. Today countries formally tagged "Emerging Markets" are considered "Developing Markets" featuring a huge new middle class. This has opened Global Markets to the imports of luxury items which only a more effluent Western Market knew. It doesn't seem that much has changed in the last twenty years. There still stands a huge demand for educated young people.

August 1993

As we've mentioned before, a reading of Alvin Toffler's *Power Shift* a year ago cleared up for me some of the different happenings in our country. Toffler believes we're changing from an industrial smoke stack economy to an information age which with this change came a great deal of pain.

We're caught up in a perennial gale of creative destruction. Chicago economist Joseph Schumpter described it: "We have much innovation occurring with new products replacing old ones. When this happens people are out of work". **(Does this sound familiar after listening to recent political debates in 2012?) How many of your friends and acquaintances are in the "information" business?**

Ninety years ago more than 50 percent of our population worked in agriculture. Today, it's less than 4 percent. What happened to all of those people? We're asking the same question now as computers replace people.

One common drum beat is that while businesses are downsizing and becoming more streamlined and more productive, our government is trailing miserably. We believe that within the next decade, Washington must be awakened by the new movement being led by American industry and begin to downsize our government as corporations have. IBM will lay off an additional 35,000 next year (1994). Procter & Gamble says goodbye to 15,000…Even while it's a profitable company, its CEO says, "We're going to take this company apart brick by brick and rebuild it." This is a sign of the times… Creative Destruction.

September 1993

"Journalists or Financial Advisors…."
One of the problems a professional financial advisor faces is that many magazine and newspaper writers are acting as investment advisors. Most of these "experts" have nothing to give to the potential investor that comes from anything other than journalism school. Recently it was pointed out to us that the sole experience in finances of one of the financial writers in the Dallas/Fort Worth metroplex was the 6 years he had spent as an editor of a major newspaper's food section.

One third of the people who put together the summer edition of *Money Magazine's* Money Guide have never purchased a mutual fund and less than half of them own more than one fund. This was disclosed by *Money's* assistant managing editor Tyler Mathisen, in his editor's notes.

Most financial writers are mainly journalists. Many of them have worked for other publications unrelated to the investment industry. Richard Burgheim, for example, covered heavy metal rock bands for *People Magazine* as preparation for advising investors at *Money*.

Burgheim seems to know how not to pay a stock broker. He always advises readers to buy no load funds, but dumb enough to lose 20% of his money in a no load gold fund last year, as he admitted in a recent article. Any competent broker would have told Burgheim that gold has more volatility than a rock and roll base guitarist (maybe he would have understood). So if you're taking your investment advice from *Money Magazine*, you're taking advice from a journalist, not an expert.

Observation – Current
(Looks like our Mr. Burgheim took a knife to a gun fight.)

Continuing…

The next time you read one of the popular financial magazines, *Forbes*, *Money*, et al., turn through its pages and make a quick estimate of the advertising dollars spent by the no-load funds in those publications. And then remember when the markets go south, and they always do, just try to find one of those journalist investment advisors who tell you what to do. Based on the years of experience we've had, we think you'll find them assigned back to the travel section, or better still to the section that tries to explain the Clinton health plan.

December 1992
Observation – Current

Prepare to hear the same old story we hear before every Presidential Election: "What happens if…?"

There have probably been more words written about what will happen, when Clinton becomes President, than any other single item since the election. One group says that interest rates will go up, so "get out of long term bonds." Another group says that particular environmental stocks and companies that would profit by an infrastructure overhaul would be the place to go.

We believe that your look should be long term. We believe that the same philosophy of utilizing professional money managers and taking careful inventory of your risk tolerance will lead you to where you want to go. Jumping in and out of the market has not been a successful ploy for many. Records confirm that, generally, the Administration in power has little to do with stock market results.

November 1992
From a New York Times Opinion Editorial

… A lot of perspective clients are telling us—"the Republican policies kept the stock market afloat during the 1980s; now that there is a change; we want to go slow on investing for a while."

There are undeniable differences between Democrats and Republicans that usually find their way into a wide range of policy decisions. Historically, Republican administrators tend to favor and protect those who have managed to succeed, while the Democrats purport to create opportunity for those who have not yet tasted success. Republican presidents tend to favor deregulation of large companies and view the Blue Chip firms as a national treasure to be protected and guarded. Democratic presidents prefer to regulate the larger companies to protect the public (not to mention labor unions and other big contributors). They attempt to improve the competitive environment for smaller firms which (right or wrong) they view as a key to greater employment, innovation, and… to use the current Democratic buzz word… change.

Observation – Current

The only difference now is that we have staggering debt and a shell shocked Senate, House, and Administration and our debt is distributed to world wide sovereign countries—not just our own citizens/Bond holders.

Observation – Current

This was true in 1992 and remains true. The only difference is it seems that in present culture that people running for President of the United States (as well as the Senate and Congress) attempt to tell people what they want to hear. Oh, for the day when a patriot steps to the microphone and tells us the truth!

Further Observations

In case you're confused, this was before the Tea Party and the Occupy Wall Street crowd began to speak.

Occasionally over the years, we wrote articles for our website. Here's one that was inspired by a longtime colleague from a monthly newsletter.

Here are some investment danger zones.

We see an introduction to sure trouble. Here's a sample: "Fed Sees Recovery Lagging", "Bernanke Says, Growth Slower Than Expected," "Monetary Policy Isn't Panacea," "Faded Malls Leave Cities In The Lurch...," "Europe Wrestles With Solutions For Greek Debt Crisis," "Brazil President's Chief Of Staff Resigns Amidst Scandal."

One thing about these crises is that nobody knew they were going happen and most of us look at them in a negative way, as tragedy. Interesting enough, other "bear market made crises" will sprout up by the time you read this. Bad things are going happen.... or they are not. There is also a possibility that investments will decline in value as each of these "crises" comes to a head; then they'll regain the temporarily lost value, once each "crisis" is resolved.

We see the proper response to these bear markets as purely counterintuitive. Basically this means that great financial advice in general, such as we hope to be able to give you, would suggest you do the opposite of what you feel is emotionally right. Great advice is precisely the opposite of what people expect and desperately want to hear."

When people yearn to bet the ranch on some brilliant new technology which has been a hot market sector for several years, we would tell them, "Don't do it". "Stay diversified". When clients insist on bailing out of a tail-spinning market, we not only tell them to stand fast, we suggest that they should buy more, This does not come from emotion, this advice comes from a historical study of the markets worldwide."

While we believe there are alternative investments which can help temper the down turns, all bear markets end in the start of a bull market when it comes to averages. One thing you can bet on, we will have another bear market; when, or it's duration, no one knows. And when we do, ask yourself if you welcome it as an opportunity to have your managers make some excellent buys of stocks on sale, or do you become panicky and yearn to bail out?"

We hope you recognize this paragraph is just another short comment on Behavioral Finance.

Much of this essay came from Nick Murray Interactive, Volume II issue August 2011.[†]

And now flashing back to 1972

In a recent survey of people's attitudes towards mutual funds, the Investment Company Institute pointed out that out of the 63 mil-

---

lion households in the U.S., 92% do not own funds...70% don't know anything about funds.

Higher Taxes?

"Yes," says our Washington contact, "but not until after elections. Sensible economists know that you can't keep spending more than you take in even if you are the United States Government..."

(The economists have been saying this for forty years!)

Kiplinger Reports...
"...That 13% of the population doesn't have enough to meet what the government calls a minimum adequate level of living. For a non-foreign family of four the needed income to reach that standard is $3,968 a year."

Observation – Current
That figure has increased since 1972. So much for inflation. And, fund ownership—Now more than 50% of American families are stock investors.

April 1994

Oh Horrors, a down market!

Considering the number of clients and the amount of money we have under management, we've had very few phone calls regarding the recent downturn in the markets. With this sell off it is an excellent time to review with our readers the concept of professional management, especially in the area of "value investing." Probably 85% to 90% of the money we have under management at Omega is in the hands of value investor managers.

So what's the difference?

Value investors buy companies not markets. Basically here is what they say: 'Do we like this company? Do we like what they make or service? Where are their markets? What future plans do they have? In what position are they in their niche? Let's visit the management and look at their operation. Let's find out if we would like to own this company, not just stock during some Bull market, but the company itself. In other words do we want to rent the stock of this company or own it?

During rising markets momentum will take good and bad company stocks upward. During down turning or bear markets both good and bad company stocks also go down. A value investor after agreeing that he likes the company, analyzes the balance sheet and decides what the company is worth, let's say, $20 a share. He then goes to the market place and possibly in the market place, the shares are priced at $32.

In this scenario, the value investor walks away from the market but does not walk away from the company. He believes it is too expensive at $32.

Easy for you to say.

Continuing research keeps the value investor up to date on the progress of the company he likes. He is only waiting for the market to bring the price of the shares down so that he can have a buying opportunity. Thus, your invested dollars in stable hands, anticipates, looks for, and hopes for down turning markets so shares can be bought at bargain prices.

A downturn in the market scares the public but not the professional. Sooner or later the market itself recognizes the value of the company and by continuing to research and monitor the activities of the company; the value investor has a pretty good idea when to sell the shares (he may not ever sell if the company remains a good one). He reaps the benefits of the capital appreciation and later, dividend payments.

So those of us who own mutual fund shares representing money being managed as described above, should not fret about 'the sky is falling' excitement generated by the media. It is this panic that causes amateurs and inexperienced professionals to dump shares at precisely the wrong time.

Americans are curiously funny; we shop the entire county for bargains on automobiles, clothes and jewelry. Yet we feel good about buying our securities at the highest prices and selling them at the lowest possible price (fear is an emotion that can't defeat faith). Ring up another victory for investment advisors who work with their clients, analyze their risk perimeters and set about to stand with their clients during the times when other people panic.

Observation – Current
The most valuable investment guide you can obtain is a dedicated, courageous, and honest advisor who prevents you from jumping off the ledge when the markets swoon!

May 1994

The Penalty of in and out investing...

In a recent quantitative analysis of investor behavior conducted by the DALBAR Financial Services, INC., we found some interesting statistics passed on to us by the Pasadena Group of mutual funds in their most recent quarterly bulletin.

From 1983 through 1993, the S&P 500 Stock Index with dividends reinvested returned 293%. During this same period the returns of surveyed equity mutual fund investors showed only 70 percent to 90 percent gains. Why? While many fund managers failed to "beat the market," this was not the correct answer. According to DALBAR the answer was poor market timing on the part of investors. Money cannot grow unless it stays invested for the entire period. Investment return appears to be far more dependent on investor behavior than fund performance.

Other major findings from the DALBAR study include:

Sales force advised investors outperformed direct market investors (1-800-no help) by over 20 percent in equity and 14 percent in fixed income funds. The advantage is directly traceable to longer retention periods and reduced reaction to changes in market conditions.

Trading in mutual funds reduces investment returns. The buy and hold strategy outperforms the average investor by more than three to one after ten years.

More investors are making the wrong choice about the method of investing in mutual funds. The market share of assets in direct marketed funds (Vanguard, Fidelity, T. Rowe Price, et al.) has increased in segments where direct market investment managers perform worse, and has declined where advisor sponsored market managers perform best.

And Now the Good News…1994

Recent investor behavior shows a trend toward more stable markets. Investors' historical behavior has been to buy when markets rise and sell when there is a decline. This pattern has diminished since 1990 and is being replaced by less volatile behavior.

Observation – Current

Let's hope so…But don't bet on it!

October 1995

"Joe, this time it's different…isn't it?"

One of the problems we have in the securities business is to convince our clients that the "this time it's different" argument will not hold up.

"This time it's different" says that in up markets the market will continue to go up. "This time it's different" says that in down turning markets the stock prices will never go back up.

We have had an unprecedented bull market in this country in the 1980s and 1990s: More than 90% of today's stock fund assets have come in since the onset of this market. On top of that, half of all the stock fund assets have come in during the last 30 months.

What we all must do is to prepare our minds to understand that the market will go down. However, it is important that investors understand that the thing not to do, during these downturns, is change funds. What we must do is change our attitudes which will change our minds.

And to continue…

What you should fear is being out of the market when the Dow goes to 10,000, which is going to happen as sure as you were born. What is a 25% correction of today going to mean 30 years from now? Incidentally, the Investment Company of America reports life expectancy for a 65 year old has increased from 8 years to more than 15 years in the last 2 decades This means that you'll probably need your money longer in the future.

We aren't selling. We are buying every month, whether it's with dividend reinvestment or with new money. If the market's next 25% move is up, that's great. If the market's next 25% move is south, that's spectacular. We're a winner either way.

So, this time it's different", simply won't play. We need to get ready for the next move…. Mentally, whether it's up 10% to 20% or whether it's down 10% to 20%. Better not get excited because it's going to happen.

Here's my prescription for investing:
    1. Give your money to an experienced, consistently productive, long term thinking, professional money manager.

2. Cancel your subscription to Money magazine.

3. Never watch CNN during the day.

4. Believe nothing that comes from talking heads on CNBC.

July 1995

"…Son, Just Put That On My Visa Card…"

Probably the best description of the debt our nation has amassed appeared in a recent church bulletin. I would like to repeat it here.

Suppose you have an income of $125,760 from money you didn't work for, that comes from the contributions of all your friends and relatives who do work; however, you budget to spend $146,060. Since you don't have the money, you charge the $20,300 difference to your credit card. By the way, you already have an unpaid balance of $452,248, which when added to the new debt, comes to $472,548 on which you pay interest daily. In 1994 the Congress of the United States of America did exactly that if you multiply the above number by 10 million.

If that doesn't bring it home, nothing will.

…More from 1995…

There's something strange in Washington, D.C. water…

People complain most about government mismanagement of Social Security Assets. Surveys show that about 68% say, 'The government is mismanaging the Social Security program by investing in government IOU's." Yet, only about 47% of our national leaders think the use of surplus funds to buy Treasury Bills with Social Security assets is a serious problem. As a note here, our leaders don't understand that the purchase of government paper is buying a bond from a bankrupt institution. This political thinking is almost as ridiculous as the liberal spin that Federal giveaway programs represent an investment.

Continuing 1995

"But Buffie, we can't afford another BMW. We need to prepare for the future."

Most of us in the investment business believe that the baby boomers are saving only about a third of what they will need to fund retirement. However, we have also discovered that when people reach that magic 5-0 age, they begin consuming less and saving more. I might mention that in 1996 and 1997 a massive number of people will reach age 49. When this happens I think that we will see the savings rate increase. With an increase percentage of income being saved, we should see interest rates go down and an expansion of our economy. While there will be less consumption in the U.S., it is our opinion that this will greatly increase export companies that provide products to emerging markets such as China, India, et al, the products and services these people have never had or experienced.

March 1991

"What would happen if I really knew what the market was going to do?"

One fundamental weakness in most people when it comes to investing is being able to distinguish fluctuation from loss. If an account declined 20%, many people would figure they'd had a 20% loss and they need to be wary. They would probably watch CNBC every hour. Well, this is what causes high blood pressure and eventually the big mistake. "Do I get out, do I stay in? Maybe it'll go up 20%; maybe it'll go down another 20%."

Suppose I actually did know what the market was going to do. Let's just say I knew the market was going to go to 6,000 by May of 1996. There are some questions I'd need to ask. "What would I know that I didn't already know? It's obviously going to 6,000 at some point anyway. When it gets to 6,000 what will I do? Will I sell? If I do, I risk missing the move to 10,000. And that is the big mistake. If I could figure out what was going to happen next—as opposed to knowing what was ultimately going to happen—I'd really know when to sell."

As Don Meredith once said:

> *"Yeah, and if 'ifs' and 'buts' were candy and nuts, we'd all have a Merry Christmas!"*

"You see, I've given my money to professional managers. I don't kid myself that I know better when to sell than they do. When I become dissatisfied with my managers and figure I'm smarter than they are, then I need to manage my own money, which is a real chore." Have you really tried it for a meaningful period? If you haven't, don't!

According to our friend, Nick Murray from a Monthly Letter…
"This adventure would require that I subscribe to *Money Magazine* and a plethora of other publications which will show me the best mutual funds for the last 3 hours and 27 minutes. They'll be able to tell me the best ones to buy for the next 720 hours, since that's when the magazine comes out again."

I think I'll just pass, thank you.

March 1995

"…I'll have the prime rib and Caesar salad…but cut the tip"
Only recently I had lunch with a new acquaintance and prospective client. Since he did not want to be obligated to do business with Omega he insisted on buying lunch. During the course of our conversation he alerted me that he had in excess of $250,000 to invest but that he simply would not pay the one time 2.5% sales charge associated with the mutual funds that I presented to him. Although it's difficult for me to admit that I didn't convince him to buy, I must tell you that later I found out this man chose to go direct and purchase mutual funds from a 1-800 number. As we were leaving the table, I noticed that he had utilized a credit card to pay the check. He gave the waiter a nice 20% tip. Smiling to myself,

I reflected that he could have had my services "from here on in" for only 2.5%, plus .68% annual management fee.

Incidentally, the "no-load" funds he was considering charges no "up front" commissions, but the expense ratio or "hidden" cost average 2.25% per year. This translates for 5 years to a total of 11.25%. His "cost" would have been 11.25% over 5 years; in ten years that's 22.5% vs. 9% with us.

Who says there's no such thing as a free lunch? I enjoyed mine. The waiter liked the 20% tip. And my prospect thought he'd made a good deal.

Some business is just not worth having.

Incidentally: The fund this guy bought has since merged with two others to avoid closing its doors and is no longer listed in _The Wall Street Journal_, or any other publication available.

> **January 1996**
> **Observation – Current**
> _Most people have little understanding of the "style" or "type" of mutual fund they own. Over a half century we've seen people not worry as to the style of the manager. In lots of cases if the fund is "down" for a year, that's bad. If it's up "it's good."_

There's more to it than that. So here is the value story once again, only in a shorter more concise form.

A majority of the funds our clients own are managed by value type managers (bargain hunters). By holding their stocks for the long term, these managers easily make up for short term disappointments. This class of funds in a Morningstar's study kept their portfolios fairly stable with the annual turnover running about 20% below average. A slower trading pace allows time for undervalued stocks to be recognized by the market and also minimizes transaction costs. Perhaps most important, it helps prevent whipsaw—the danger of reacting to a sudden move in the market just in time for its reversal. Haven't we all experienced that?

Where did you work in 1987?

And here's another thing we've discovered. Today the average diversified equity/stock/ mutual fund has had the same manager for only 3½ years, but managers who have consistently beaten the S&P 500 have been running their funds for an average of 10 years. The tenure of the managers who handle 90% of the money Omega Securities oversees is 14½ years. (in 1996).

Holding funds for the long term, investing with conviction, buying on weakness, and focusing on the best management are all attributes of the successful professional money manager as well as the successful investor.

> ### Observation – Current
> *Presently the majority of our managers have tenure of over 24 years. (as of 2012)*

November 1996

Recently a number of publications have crossed my desk which, if received by our clients, I hope they ignore. These publications address the question of the cost of buying mutual fund shares. The media dotes on the no-load fund concept and one of our local columnists at the *Fort Worth Star Telegram* even gives (800) numbers for his no-load favorites along with his recommendations.

The problem here, as I see it, equates to giving a loaded gun to an untrained eight year old. Most people don't have the foggiest when it comes to judging risk vs. reward, and just because it's free doesn't make it good. Most publications today try to intimidate readers who utilize real-life professional advisors rather than a 1-800-NO-HELP phone call. "Hold it right there, Buster!"

We've observed that there are certain people who want to handle their own investment planning and believe they do not need the help of a professional. This article is not addressed to them (however, we would advise these people that they should include their spouse in all of their planning; educate him/her; be sure that he/she is computer oriented and enjoys managing money as much as his/her spouse. You know—we don't live forever).

June 2000

According to *Morningstar,* one hundred seventy seven funds posted 1999 returns of more than 100%. From 1989 to 1998 only ten funds could claim an annual return of 100% or more in any one year. Five funds in 1993 and five in 1998 posted 100% + return. **Recent surveys have said that newer investors have expectations to have a return of 20% or more over the next 10–15 years.** "You wish—You dream!"

Observation – Current

This leads us to believe that individuals who have invested in a Bull Market foolishly think that the market itself will make up for their not investing their own money. And when we run into flat or down periods we'll have literally thousands of people approaching retirement with tears in their eyes since the market hasn't treated them the same way it treated them during the 90s.

December 2000

"If you are feeling good about things, read this."

These pages have shown and quoted that the top 1% of Americans pays more tax than the majority pays, but let me make this clear. We're not saying that the top 1% pays the majority of the tax. What we are saying is something a little different. A tiny fraction of Americans pay more tax than a majority, (which can elect the government). The very structure of a democratic government as known in the early days of the 21st century makes *pillage* an almost inevitable feature of tax policy. There will not be a keen majority for cutting taxes in a country like the United States, when about a thousand households will receive more of the benefit of lower taxes than the poorest 66 million households. It would require a political miracle for the system to willingly permit the 1% of Americans who pay most of the taxes to keep more of what they earn. Rather, the side who wants to reduce debt first, then take a tax cut are the same people who, when offered a raise at their place of employment say: "No, I'd rather you reduce company debt first, then if there's any thing left, you can give me a raise." Don't you believe it.

Observation – Current

There are countless examples of the wisdom of cutting taxes to increase government revenue. It is so obvious that, as you read political and economic history, you wonder how anyone would believe that raising taxes in order to stimulate the economy is anything less than IDOITIC. Lowering taxes (especially taxes on dividends and capital gains) encourages diversification by using profits made from a sale to spread over other different investments; giving the investor the freedom to make his own decisions to sell, buy, or hold.

January 2002

Many people reading their third quarter 2001 reports on their mutual funds wished they hadn't opened their mail. Indeed, during the third quarter the S&P 500 and the Morgan Stanley World Index are among the worst quarterly performance results experienced in recent memory.... The NASDAQ's 30.6% decline was by far the worst by any of the major indices as technology and related stocks were painfully hard hit stocks....Things were much better in the fourth quarter, although many funds were down for the year....

Spring 2002

"Don't tax me, don't tax thee, tax that man behind the tree."
"Tax the rich! They never pay enough taxes."

Were you aware that the top one percent of all earners in 1999 earned 19.5% of all adjusted gross income reported to the IRS, yet they paid 32.2% of all federal income taxes that year? YEP! The "super rich" pay in taxes nearly double their proportion of national income. It's easy to see who is financing this government. About twenty years ago the "super-rich" paid only 19% of all federal income taxes. By 1991 that share had climbed to 24.8% and by 1999 it was above 36%. The story is the same for the merely "filthy-rich", the top 5% of filers, who according to *The Wall Street Journal*, paid 43.4% of all taxes in 1991, but by 1999 paid 55.5%. (The comment key here was the 15% capital gains tax rate instigated by the Reagan Administration).

We wonder how the government will make it since the top income tax rate has been cut from 39.6% to 35%. However, maybe we can squeeze by for a while because that doesn't go into effect until 2006.

"Who are the wealthy?"
According to *The Wall Street Journal* and the 1999 IRS numbers, all you had to earn to be among the top 25% of all tax filers was a whooping $52,965. To be among the top 50% you had to earn only $26,415. The interesting thing about this number is that many of these average people are tomorrow's wealthy. According to an analysis of the University of Michigan for the period from 1975-1991, more than 80% of the families who started in the lowest 1/5 of earning population, had moved to middle-class incomes, earning an average $22,304 or above that last year of 1991.

"Dividends. Ah! How sweet the sound! (LOUDER PLEASE)"

As we've mentioned in these pages, we believe that the dividend tax break offered by the Bush Administration should go to the companies and not investors. As an example, in the year 2000, the S&P 500 companies paid out just a third of their reported earnings as dividends. This means that those earnings after taxes are still resting in the confines of the corporate structure. Make no mistake—we need some sort of change. Money paid out as dividends is currently taxed twice, at both the corporate and at the individual level. That has two unsavory consequences.

"Proceed Sir!"

First, companies that need money to grow tend to borrow, rather than utilize cash. The reason, of course, is that the companies can take a tax deduction for the interest they pay, but they don't get any tax break for paying dividends. What is really happening is that the tax code is encouraging companies to load up on debt. That's not exactly a recipe for economic stability... And of course, the tax code also gives top executives incentive to hang onto profits and use the money to gun for faster growth in an effort to bolster their companies' share price. Why? Under present law, if a company kicks off a dividend, both the corporation and shareholders pay taxes on the money involved. The top executives would rather increase the share price to coincide with the stock options they were given to increase the value of the companies' stock. So what is the answer? Who knows?

"Whatever the answer is, we need to stop double taxing dividends"

Summer 2004

Reflections on the First Forty

Comments

When you think of it, 40 years is a long time. In fact, my biblical studies have shown me that it represents a generation. Well, my 40th Anniversary in the financial business is coming up in July. Besides the obvious "Thanks" to everybody who has helped us along the way, I will say that I never would have dreamed that 40 years would have turned out this way. I'll not make the mistake of telling you that I plan on retiring because that isn't a consideration. But 40 years is an excellent milestone that gives me a chance to reflect a little on some of the things that have happened along the way.

While I began my career on a part-time basis in 1962, I came full-time with the *"Financial Advisory Clinic"* in 1964. In those days, there were very few of us who were what we called, "dually licensed," cleared to sell insurance and also securities.

In November of 1963, we suffered the tragedy of President Kennedy's assassination. 1964 and 1965, we were struck with the revelation of the Civil Rights marches and as the 60s progressed, we watched the Vietnam War escalate. By 1967, we were in a nice up- market despite the riots in Newark, NJ and our country suffering more and more with the conflict in Vietnam. We were busy then working with helicopter pilots in Mineral Wells, Texas, helping them accumulate assets for the future as they did their duty in that terrible war.

In 1969, we underwent a downturn caused by tight money as the market fell and on into the early 70s as Cambodia was invaded. We went through the wage-price freeze and sadly, Watergate, where we watched the televised proceedings. We were unable to realize that this was a portent of things to come.

Our securities business suffered in the years '73–'74 during the oil embargo and during the scandals of the Nixon presidential administration. Those years were tough, as many of you know. (Today. those are the years that we review hypothetical illustrations to show you the worst years in the last few decades.)

And… Oh! Curse the day we went off the gold standard! (Well, there are many attitudes about the gold standard!)

Things snapped back in '75, as our troops were withdrawn from Vietnam. It was then we became involved with the Southern Medical Association Retirement Plan and began to expand our markets through the southern states and Eastern Seaboard.

Our relationship with this physician group lasted 20 years.

Do you remember when New York City almost went bankrupt? The market continued to rise in 1976 in spite of the New York crisis.

There were many reasons not to invest in the '70s and probably the main reason was the energy crisis. However, those of us who did, and have held on, have discovered that the wait was worth it. We ushered the 80s in, as well as President Ronald Reagan.

"Time marches on…"

It was 1983 when I purchased, what is now Omega Securities, from World Service Life Insurance Company, here in Fort Worth. Little did we know that we were coming into the business with our own brokerage firm at the beginning of the broadest, most exciting, bull market in history. Talk about "tail wind"! Many clients came with us during those heady times, riding the Bull Market. And only a few left after the internet bubble burst and 9-11 awakened the world with a new war. Those who stayed, incidentally, have watched their accounts come back in beautiful fashion.

Since we had been through the '73–'74 market, at the end of the 90s the bear market did not affect us psychologically as much as those grueling years in the early 70s. So, we are now back on the upside as has always happened. The economic turn-around has continued to remind us that a democratic government coupled with a free market society will always win in the long run.

Finally, when our clients began to wonder about the future and my longevity, John Dickens joined us in 2000, Tom Hardgrove in 2001, and Tammy Bryant celebrated her 10th year in 2003. All three are now partners. The future looks good (and young!). **The story always get better!**

So what else has that generation of 40 years brought?

If an observer analyzed the performance of one of our favorite funds, Investment Company of America, he would discover that in those 40 years there were only 6 negative 12 month periods. 34 winners and 6 losses are not too bad.

The family who invested $10,000 in ICA with full sales charge on my second day on the job, July 16, 1964, and had the courage to hold on would have seen on March 31, 2004, their account with a value of $931,527.*

On the other hand a $10,000 investment in the S&P 500 Stock Index would have grown to $507,777 by March 31, 2004.**

My friend, Kevin Clifford, President of American Fund Distributors, when asked about what to do when there are so many thousands of mutual funds out there—how do you decide which ones to buy? Kevin gave an old Kentucky horseman's answer,

"When there are too many horses, you got to bet on the jockeys."
This is what we have done. We are convinced that you, our clients, are well positioned with your investments in the American Funds. We've spent 40 years checking the jockeys. The ones you have are the best!

More later...
In winding down this emotional odyssey, I'll steal a line or two from Garth Brooks (with apologies!)

> "Yes, I could have left my life to chance.
> I would have surely missed the pain,
> But I'd also missed the Dance."

Mid Winter 2008

"The Piper is being paid—guess who writes the biggest check"
At least once a year we appreciate *The Wall Street Journal's* coverage of the Congressional Budget Office and the IRS in releasing tax numbers for the last two years (2005). One of the more interesting parts of the news is that the richest 1% of the income earners paid about 39% of all income taxes that year. The richest 5% paid a little less than 60% and the richest 10% carried 70% of the burden.

According to the Journal article, if your income was below the median—half of all households—you paid a mere 3% of all income taxes in 2005. The richest 1.3 million tax filers—those Americans with adjusted gross incomes of more than $305,000—paid more of the income tax than all of the 66 million American tax filers below the median income which was 10 times more.

The best way that we can figure, the Democrat Presidential hopefuls whom all stated that they will increase the taxes on the rich, will attempt to out-tax President Bush. This will be a tough task. Based on the latest available tax data, no Administration in modern history has done more to pry tax revenue from the wealthy than the Bush administration. The share of the income taxes paid by the top 5% of the income earners has increased quite rapidly. Interestingly enough, despite tax reductions in 2001 and 2003, the "rich" saw their share of taxes paid rise at a faster rate than their share of income.

"Define risk… Please!"

So when you start defining "rich", how do you describe a senior couple, middle class, who have lived modestly for decades, suddenly retires and sells the family business or home for $1 million or more? These people may be "rich" in a Presidential hopeful's definition of the term, but in fact they are benefiting in one tax year from a lifetime of hard work and thrift. Are these people really "rich"?

We could go on and on into the capital gains situation. According to a government report, "The amount of capital gains declared on tax forms has doubled since the tax rate was cut to 15% from 20% in 2003, which has also contributed to more Americans being rich. Dividend income has also increased by 50% since that rate was cut to 15% from nearly 40% in 2003. Part of the income gains of the "rich" are simply a result of assets which have been converted into taxable income in part because of lower tax rates.

We are sorry if we upset our friends **running to the left of us**, but if the Democrats really want to soak the rich they will keep the tax rates where they are by extending the Bush tax cuts…or better still, lower them some more.

Why I saved a 1998 article, I can't explain.

The Thursday, July 2, 1998 op-ed page of *The Wall Street Journal* had an interesting article by Mark Helpren, novelist and a contributing editor to that publication. In discussing the Clinton Administration he points out that it is difficult for individuals or nations to recognize that war and peace alternate. No matter how long peace may last it will end in war. Though most people cannot believe at this moment that the United States of America will ever again fight for its survival, history guarantees that it will. When war comes again most people will not know what to do. They will, of course, believe of war as they did of peace: that it is everlasting. Mr. Helpren goes on to show that the "Statesman" who is different from the "Politician" must, in the midst of common despair see the end of war, just as during the peace he was alive to the inevitably of war. The Politician will revel with his people and enjoy their enjoyments. The Statesman however, in continual stress of soul, will think of destruction. As others move in the light, he'll move in darkness. So that as others move in darkness that he may move in the light.

"So how does this affect me now?"

It has suddenly occurred to me that this is the position that we've taken for many years. When markets and the economy are good, we've always told you in these paragraphs that downturns are going to come. Just as sure as war follows peace, Bear markets follow Bull markets. This is one of the most difficult things we face as investment advisors: we must always remind you that if you haven't been in the stock market in 1973 and 1974 you really haven't seen a Bear market.

As valuations of domestic stocks increase (this means they become more and more overpriced as compared to their earnings) we approach closer and closer to a downturn in this domestic market. Convincing our clients of this is the job we've taken on. It's been fairly easy during most of the nineties, since the market has treated

*us so well. But these are the times when you need investment help
more than any time.*

October 2000

Volatility

It seems that everyday the stock market ride is like a plane flight on
a stormy night and one engine flames out; the oxygen masks drop
down; everybody gets into the crash position, but shortly thereafter
the aircraft lands safely and everyone escapes with minor injuries.

If this volatility that we have seen in the market leaves you sick to
your stomach, then maybe we should consider having you get on
a train next time. If as investors (that includes this writer) we are
shocked by the volatile days we have seen almost all summer, we
either have to learn more about markets or check our portfolios
and get into a more conservative stance. **Panicking during volatile
times causes people to make all the wrong decisions.**

"Are you telling me I should not sell when my funds go down?"

During these times, it is important to stay with whatever long term
strategy one has adopted. If like so many people, you have not
adopted one, now is a good time to do it. While it is difficult to do
so, we would encourage our clients to think in terms of decades.
Just a few years ago the average investor held a stock fund for about
10 to 12 years. Today the average holding period is less than 3 years,
according to the Investment Company Institute. Of course, this
takes into consideration the 401(k) plans and other qualified retirement programs that allows investors to shift from fund to fund
without paying taxes. But from our standpoint, we can also blame
the media.

"You mean investing is R-rated?"

If you do a quick review of prime time TV you will discover that
it is all about emergency rooms and police shows. The television
producers make people believe that everyone is caught up in this

life and death drama when most people's lives are mundane. The same should be true about how most people invest: long term and very unexciting. Your morning newspaper, CNBC, CNN, and other financial publications all want your rapt attention; thus they employ headline writers, columnists and show hosts who do everything to get your attention. They want you to rely on them for investment advice. The problem here, of course, is that when they give bad advice that you follow and lose your shirt, your complaints mean nothing. Not so with your NASD and SEC regulated Investment Advisor. I dare say (while I have no proof) that more money has been lost following the advice of the media than all the Ponzi schemes ever invented.

"So… you have some suggestions?"

We would suggest that when you get your quarterly report from your fund company, and/or us, during the first part of October, you take a look at where you are and let us know if you would like to set up time to have a meeting. Diversifying the portfolio reduces risk and evens out the overall return, which makes you less likely to sell in a panic.

October 2000

A Vote For International
Comments from John Dickens

For the last six months, Joe and I have stressed to new and current clients the need for a global/international position in all portfolios. Our approach going forward into this new millennium is that all accounts should have at least a 30% position in global and international funds. If the U.S. market is flat over the next year or so we need to be in other parts of the world to make up the difference.

"Is the U.S. market overpriced?" Some people think so. Jim Bianco of Bianco Research reports that in August 1929, the total market capitalization of U.S. stocks equaled just over 81% of GDP. When less than 500 companies are valued at more than 80% of the value of all the goods and services exchanged in the economy, something is out of whack, that something being investor confidence in the necessity and desirability of buying stocks.

In November 1968 and again in December 1972 the market capitalization of the stock market soared to 77.3% and 78% of GDP, respectively. And again, both times, the value of stocks fell dramatically, reverting to their historic mean of around 50% of GDP.

So what, you may ask, is the ratio of market cap to GDP now? In June, it was 165%. Investors valued stocks at over $16.3 trillion while nominal GDP was $9.9 trillion. Herein lies the cancer in the American market: too many dollars chasing too few earnings. Are the future earnings of all publicly traded companies currently worth more than twice the value of all economic activity in this country?

We don't know the answer, but we do know that you can't have all your money in U.S. funds right now. You need to be diversified and have a healthy international position. "Call—we can help…"

March 2001

"Take the long way to success."
While we all seem to be on the same page when it comes to the long term view of investment tracking, I've decided that long term projections of budget surpluses, especially for 10 years, is tough to justify.

The problem of course is that it's very hard to believe that we'll go ten years without a recession. When that happens, tax revenues plunge and the surpluses disappear, or at least they diminish. Naturally Washington's answer when the money gets short is to raise taxes. (Wrong) A future Congress can change the tax structure when it gets ready. The idea that the lowered tax rate recommended by the Bush administration will continue for ten years is hard to swallow. His idea to lower taxes prior to a budget agreement is good. Give Americans back the overcharge and let Washington learn to live with the rest.

This does not mean that we do not favor a tax cut. That's coming for sure, but with the Devil being in the details. We find out now that (based on first writing) most of it won't kick in for several years.

"But here is the real problem."
If Congress does not stop the rapid growth of government, however, a tax cut will only lead to where we were in the early 80's when we all worked a little harder as our tax dropped to 28% and Washington continued to throw money at useless targets.

"So what else is needed?"
As we wrote in our last *Opinions & Facts*, if we really wanted to add to the surplus, we would either reduce or eliminate the capital gains tax. Some experts tell us that there is

$20 trillion in unrealized gains frozen in people's stock portfolios. If you cut the capital gains tax rate in half (20% to 10%) we could encourage re-investment and collect a ton of money while helping get rid of recession. **(And believe me, we are on the cusp of a recession.)** This is the key to truly financing the existing Technology Revolution; after-tax money, not leveraged dollars.

"So What About Recession?"
Of course what happens in hard times is that you get better service. When there is competition and people discover they either have to work or lose their jobs, you'll find an improved economy and an increasing gross domestic product.

Please feel free to *react* **rather than** *resist*.

So bring on the tax cuts. But don't forget about slowing the spending in Washington. The Score Card for 2000…UGH!!

The Dow Jones Industrials finished the year 2000 down 6.18%, its worst calendar year since 1981.

The S&P 500 Index finished down 9.18%, its worst year since 1974. The Russell 2000 Small Cap Index was down 4.20%, the first time it's beaten the S&P 500 Index in a down year.

The NASDAQ composite was down 39.29%…its worst calendar year since inception in 1971, and it was down 53.7% from peak to trough (as of this writing it's down more than 60%).

The Wilshire 5000 total US stock market was down 10.29%…its worst calendar year since 1974.

The utilities were the best performing industry sector in the year 2000 (up 52.8%), followed by healthcare (up 36.7%) and the S&P Real Estate Investment Trust Composite was up 28.84%.

One of the clearest lessons from these facts is that anybody who chased hot performance suffered in almost precisely the proportion to the heat of the performance they were chasing. Latecomers to the tech-boom experienced one of the nastiest corrections in recent memory, while those who jumped into the S&P 500 were slapped in the face (I surrender!). Those who own diversified portfolios and refuse to believe the astronomical tech valuations sailed through this ugly bearish period without much more than a scratch.

Remember what the British say: "Keep calm and carry on!"

1989 December

"...Thank you, Mr. Casey; I know your $12.50 book will make us both rich..."

Crisis Investing by Douglas Casey

Here's a quote from a bestselling book written by a well–known investment advisor: "From 25%–50% of your total assets should be in gold and silver.... This kind of diversification should protect you from the worst financial aspects of the (coming) depression and offer the best appreciation potential.... The debacle the world is now facing will be lengthy and extensive. It should be the economic sideshow of the century, if not the millennium."

Note that this book carried a copyright of 1979.

Well, we're at that stage again. More people are telling us to get into gold, or cash, and that the future looks bleak.

Observation – Current
If we had followed Casey's advice in 1979, we would have missed the most booming and dynamic bull market in common stocks ever known.

"It reminds me of the head of the U.S. Patent Office who in 1906 recommended that the office be closed since everything that could be invented had been invented. Moral: Be careful what you say; it comes back to haunt you."

December 1990

Quote of The Month

"The market can only climb or fall forever if it is disconnected from reality. At the great market peaks and valleys, a large number of folks have come to believe that reality no longer counts, only to be destroyed by reality's return."

— David D Tripple,
Chief Investment Officer, Pioneer Fund

"1991 Marks our 30th year in the securities business. Following are a few things we've learned..."   —JEH

When down (bear) markets occur, rather than panic and run for the door, it's a good time to sit down and distinguish fear from knowledge. One of the things we've learned over the years is that just because prices go down doesn't mean values decline. On the other hand if prices of things go up, it doesn't necessarily mean that the value also goes up. In the short run almost anything can happen to prices of stocks; and some very strange things do happen. One should analyze what he owns, why he bought it, and what his "time horizon" is for holding it. Trying to "time" the market as an amateur by buying and selling on "feel" is an exercise in futility.

Most people buy individual stocks with the hope that the price will increase. There are only three things a stock price can do – and two of them are bad. If it goes up, do I sell and take my profits? If it stays level, do I get out and put my money into CDs? If it goes down, do I buy more, hold, or sell? "Flip a coin, brother."

When professional money managers buy stocks, they buy for different reasons. They buy because they have totally researched the company, the company's management, product offered, competition, and financial situation. Professionals buy for reasons other than "hope."

One thing we've tried to impress upon our clients is that when you buy mutual funds, it's not like buying a stock. What you're really doing is buying professional management. The managers make the decision as to what cash position to be in; the managers do the research on the companies whose stocks they own; the managers make the decision when to liquidate stocks. (**The mutual fund is not some nebulous thing out there that acts independently; rather it's a viable company run by professionals whose job it is to make your money grow and to protect you in down markets.**)

If you'll just think about it, most of us choose our investments between fixed or guaranteed returns and variable investments, such as stock funds. If you use the fixed, guaranteed approach (CD, annuity, etc.), you have greater asset protection in bad times but no share of growth in good times. If you select equities, you share in the growth of earnings and dividends. You are at risk if they decline in price. And you have less protection during recessionary times.

The reason that the long term investment data shows that equities have a higher return is because owners have had to work a little harder and take a little more risk.

To quote a Wall Street maxim: "There is no free lunch." The "cost of lunch" is volatility, which means that in some years equity returns will be unsustainably good and some years there will be losses. They are both part of the long term results which are much better than the return on fixed investments."

Things Discovered While Looking for Other Things…

Forbes Magazine reports that in spite of our fears that the Japanese will own America that during the last decade direct investment in the United States from the United Kingdom grew by $105 billion as against $65 billion from the supposedly dominant Japanese. By year end 1989 Europe's total investment in this country was $200 billion more than Japan's; in 1980, it was only $50 billion more….

In the opinion of Sir John Templeton, Chairman, Templeton, Galbraith and Hansberger, Ltd., international money managers, the strength of national currencies is based on the nature of the people of that country. Sir John points out that those nations whose people are more honest, thrifty and diligent have stronger currencies. He reminds us that if we want to see which nations will be the most prosperous and have the strongest currency, there are three things to study. Are the people diligent? Are they thrifty? And are they honest? These qualities, he concludes, dominate all other factors in deciding what will happen to the currency of that nation...And to conclude: **Churches and charities in America will receive in 1990 about $100 billion in donations from generous people. This is more in one nation, in one year, than the total of all donations in all nations, in any century before this one.**

June 1988

CDs And Other Dream Machines...

While reading an ad advertising interest rates for annuities and CDs, my mind raced back a quarter century. I remembered a fixed annuity ad that a major insurance company ran in all the national high-circulation magazines. It showed a guy in a boat fishing on a beautiful lake. The headline read, "How I Retired on $400 A Month."

After three or four years passed, there appeared the same ad, except now the copy read, "How I Retired on $600 A Month."

Inflation.

"I wondered what had happened to the first guy who had retired on $400."

Inflation. A problem 25 years ago. Still a problem today. Too bad those guys never understood the concept of capital growth. Fixed annuity and CD investments do not grow; the bank or insurance company simply adds interest to the principal. The original investment has no chance to increase in value.

"Don't forget the guy in the boat. He's no longer fishing for fun. Now he's fishing for his dinner."

> ### Observation – Current: 2013
>
> *We thought Phineas T. Barnum was dead, buried and forgotten. But no deal—He still lives—or at least his philosophy lives.*
>
> *There really is a sucker born every minute.*

May 1991

Think About It...

By *abstaining* from using short-term measures to reflate and stimulate economic activity, governments can help insure that future economic growth will be sustainable and non-inflationary. Sustainable economic growth is created by technological change and investment, not by artificial stimulus to demand. This technological growth, of course, is attributed to long-term research and investment...the true wellsprings of growth.

August 1991

"You Can't Tell The Players Without A Scorecard..."

Just about the time we got used to Comrade Gorbachev and learned to pronounce his name, we get some other bird claiming to be King of Russia. (At this printing, Gorby has come back from the dead and is frantically trying to hold things together.) The most knowledgeable observers have agreed that moving a totalitarian government to a free market system is not accomplished with a road map, compass and an eight-lane highway. There will be many bumps and detours before it's accomplished. Wars, rumors of same, and all that jazz.

You see, as investors we must expect to go through these things. It is only with the downturn in markets and prices of shares that professionals are tested. Nothing ever goes straight up or straight down except maybe Russian leaders. This writer believes that Eastern European and Soviet Citizens have had just enough of a taste of Democracy to continue on the road to the free market system America has enjoyed for so many years…Your patience will be rewarded."

February 1990

SOCIALISM: "Deceased in Russia: alive and well in Cuba and Washington, D.C."
If you've been reading the same stories out of Washington we have, you'll experience what Yogi Berra once described as "déjà vu all over again."

"Tax breaks for the great middle class…" "Cash refunds to families with children under 18…."

This rallying cry by the incompetents in Congress is nothing but a cover-up for the old McGovern Socialism: redistribute the wealth. And many conservatives up there are trading off a tax break on capital gains to get in on the supposed "vote harvest."

Bush and the conservatives want the long term fix that capital gains tax breaks will give us, and the liberal gang is opting for the band-aid of personal tax refunds. The main problem, of course, is that the great majority of people in this country who are eligible to vote have never been told what the term "capital gains" means.

Our public schools, woefully short on teachers and discipline, simply do not dish this kind of heavy stuff to our young. Well, what do we expect: in the extremely litigious society we live in, teachers had better not get tough, or lawsuits will fall from heaven.

But back to capital gains…

Unless the Bush Administration can weld a coalition of conservatives on both sides of the aisle in Congress and compromise on band aids and long-term fixes, it looks like we'll continue to "pork barrel" through the next 6 months.

Tax refunds for the middle class are an absolute pipe dream. Is anybody foolish enough to think that money refunded to middle income Americans who have children under 18 will generate long term benefits? Will these people who have never been taught "short term sacrifice for long term gain" use this "tax refund or break" to generate new businesses, technology and jobs for all these people out of work? NO WAY, JOSE!

And as far as all the talk on PBS about the "Greed of the 80s," give us a break. The only people we've met who didn't want a higher standard of living, better homes, nicer cars, clothes, etc., were people who have been conned by Washington into thinking they are entitled to something they don't have to work for. Washington thinks we're all stupid.

1990

Here's an excerpt from a speech which we thought you'd enjoy.
Walt the Heinous *Hydra*

> *"Our tax system, monster that it is, was born of the needs of war.*

> *"Until World War I, no country in the world envisioned marginal tax rates of 50% or even 30%, let alone the application of these rates to working-class incomes. Once in place, the oppressive tax regime of wartime was never dislodged. Various political interests kept adding to the Code to create penalties for certain kinds of behavior and incentives or others. Various economic interests sought and won exceptions. The process created hundreds of*

thousands of lobbyists, lawyers, tax accountants and pol-
iticians who jumped on the bandwagon and turned this
system into the largest single service industry in the U.S.

"We should throw away our 4,000 page Tax Code and
start anew. The top tax rate in Hong Kong, the world's
fastest-growing economy, is 15%, and it takes less than
an hour to fill out your annual tax return. A flat tax
of 13% such as Jerry Brown proposes is the kind of plan
America will have to adopt by the end of the1990s if
we are to keep pace with a world that has rediscovered
entrepreneurial capitalism."

> — Theodore J Forstmann,
> Forstmann Little & Co.,
> In a speech for the Harvard Business School.

...all who agree stand up!

Spring 2007

And Finally...spring is here...and young men's thoughts turn to...baseball!

Since most of our readers know that John Dickens, Tom Hardgrove and I descend from a long experience in the game of baseball, we hope you'll enjoy this little baseball gem.

There is a term we learned in baseball: "Run it Out." This is used to describe what a player at bat should do when he hits a pitch. Although he might be sure it will be caught in the outfield or infield he should still run as hard as he can to first base, just in case the defensive player drops the ball.

Recently we learned that there are also other reasons to "Run it Out." I was at a college baseball game a weekend ago sitting next to an Arizona Diamondback Talent Scout who was using a radar gun checking the velocity of the pitches by the pitcher. Every time a runner would hit the ball anywhere he would produce a stop watch to time the young man running to first. During one inning, I turned to the scout who had just checked a player going to first and I said, "Can that kid run?"

The young scout answered, "No, not really." And I said, "What do you mean?" He replied, "Well, I timed him. The problem; it was a fly ball to the outfield which looked like a sure out and he really slowed up before he got to first base." I said: "You mean he didn't run it out." He nodded, "Yes."

I wondered to the scout: "Do you think he would have run as hard as he could if he knew you were up here timing him?"

The scout responded, "Of course he would" and then the young scout made a comment to me which opened my eyes to a universal truth.

"If he had run it out, I'd have made that notation in my report... probably come see him again. But since he didn't...I made that note in my book."

He said, "Mr. Hardgrove, let's say a player has 4 at bats in a game and the average speed down the line from home to first is 4.5 seconds (which really isn't fast). If he runs as hard as he can... with 4 at bats, that's 18 seconds of hustle per game." The young man then said something that astonished me.

"You know, I don't know how much money you make, but I do know that the minimum wage in the Big Leagues is around $380,000 per year. Would you work as hard as you could for 18 seconds a day if you could make the money that you make now?"

Wow! Did this guy ring my bell!

What an observation! The following Monday I came back to the office and spoke to John, Tom and Tammy Bryant and asked them the question, "Why are we having the success we are having in our business?' They answered, "Because we give good service; because we treat our clients the way we want to be treated; we completely research the fund companies we use" and—any number of other positive attributes they could think of. My response was, **"What you're really saying folks, is that we always try to 'Run it Out' no matter who's checking us out."**

To end this little story we hope that no matter what your occupation is or what your hobby is, that you'll always have a tendency to "Run it Out."

We certainly will.

Thank you for your continued business, confidence and trust. And we promise to always "Run it Out" for you... and us.

That's our baseball tale. Play ball!

October 1992 Special Edition – "Almost all were scared!"

Wall Street is nervously watching the presidential election race. Stock analysts, along with the media (especially the media), are calling for caution if President Bush loses.

In discussing this situation with a national vice-president of one of our mutual fund companies, we asked each other the question, "If Bush's survival is so important to Wall Street, and, therefore, to all investors, then why is his voter popularity at an all-time low?"

Of course, the answer is clear—Americans want change. Ross Perot's return to the great race is living proof that people are definitely in the mood for change.

Our economist friend, Rick Wilson, has pointed out for months that the problem with markets during this particular election year is that Wall Street desires predictability, and with the advent of Ross Perot, that predictability is not there. The computer models utilized by securities analysts for predicting stock movements could be thrown to the wind after Perot walked in the door. To these people, Bush is a candidate of stability.

Over the past several decades, we've missed many opportunities for purchasing because of the fears generated by the media. In fact, based on actual statistics during the last 50 years the stock market has lost money only once during the second half of a Presidential election year (1948).

Because almost all of our clients are long-term investors, we thought you would appreciate seeing what happened to the market following an election year.

Presidential Election Year
Stock Performance

	Total Return During Election Year		Three Year Total Return
	July-Dec	Dec	After Election
1940	9.4%	0.0%	33.9%
1944	4.9%	3.7%	32.6%
1948	-6.1%	3.5%	94.0%
1952	9.5%	3.8%	98.8%
1956	1.1%	3.8%	43.8%
1960	3.9%	4.8%	42.2%
1964	5.4%	0.0%	25.4%
1968	5.9%	-4.0%	8.8%
1972	11.0%	1.3%	18.9%
1976	5.1%	5.4%	17.1%
1980	21.7%	-3.2%	41.4%
1984	11.6%	2.5%	64.8%
1988	6.3%	1.8%	66.2%
Avg. Total Return	**7.0%**	**1.9%**	**42.7%**
Compound Ann. Return	**14.5%**	**25.0%**	**12.6%**

Note: Total returns include reinvested dividends
Source: Tbbotson Assoc.

For three-year periods after election years, dating back to 1940, average annual returns have been a little over 12% and total returns have been 42.7%.

In addition to the fact that the market has always moved upward for the three year period following an election, our money managers are well diversified in bonds, cash, internationally, etc., to give you a much better chance of protection in the event of an unsuspected downturn.

So, where does that leave us? Our approach is that you should maintain your long term investment strategy.

We've discovered after many years that while share prices may change overnight, real values do not.

December 1992

Hear Ye! Hear Ye! Come For A Free Lunch
The Wall Street Journal also reported that Fidelity Investments' mutual fund operation is getting into the advice-giving business I also note they have taken away sales charges on a number of funds. With the additional service of furnishing "investment pros" to give investment advice and reducing charges, we know that many people will be dialing that Fidelity telephone number to get this information.

Somewhere down the line, someone said, "There is no such thing as a free lunch and when you pay nothing for something that is usually what you get...nothing." We are not advocating overcharges, but we also have observed the result of the airlines giving away their business. Many of them have gone "belly up" in other ways besides landing a 707 with the wheels retracted.

We believe that our clients want to deal with real people whom they know, people who are paid based on how the professional money managers fare; they want people who have had experience in investment counsel. We intend to stick by that philosophy and continue to be available to offer the same enthusiastic service to our clients.

March 1993 Special Edition

THERE ARE THOSE WHO WOULD HAVE US BELIEVE THAT THE ROLE OF GOVERNMENT IS TO BE INVOLVED IN BUSINESS. THIS HAS PROVEN A TREACHEROUS PATH FOR OTHER COUNTRIES THAT HAVE ATTEMPTED IT.

FROM THE CLINTON ADMINISTRATION, WE ARE HEARING SLOGANS SUCH AS "INVESTMENT IN THE INFRASTRUCTURE." THIS IS GOVERNMENT LINGO THAT SAYS "SPEND." MAKE NO MISTAKE ABOUT IT, WHEN THE GOVERNMENT SPENDS MONEY, IT'S NOT THE GOVERNMENT'S MONEY, IT'S OUR MONEY.

THE ROLE OF BUSINESS IS TO SUPPLY IDEAS, INNOVATION, AND THE CAPITAL TO MAKE OUR ECONOMY WORK. IT IS THE GOVERNMENT'S JOB TO LET BUSINESS DO THIS WHILE MAINTAINING AN ECONOMIC ENVIRONMENT IN WHICH THE DOLLAR IS STABLE, INVESTMENT IS ENCOURAGED, AND TRADE IS FREE.

IN ORDER TO KEEP THE DOLLAR STABLE, DEFICITS MUST BE BROUGHT UNDER CONTROL. THIS CANNOT BE DONE BY TAXES ALONE. CONGRESS MUST CONTROL EXPENDITURES. TO ACCOMPLISH THIS, RATE OF GROWTH OF ENTITLEMENTS MUST EITHER SLOW OR STOP. FOR MANY YEARS, MOST SENSIBLE ECONOMISTS HAVE INDICATED THAT IF WE WOULD STOP ENTITLEMENT GROWTH, THE BUDGET COULD BE BALANCED IN SHORT TIME. CONGRESS HAS NOT HAD THE COURAGE TO DO THIS AND NOW THE DEFICIT HAS GOTTEN OUT OF CONTROL.

ENTITLEMENTS NOT ONLY BUST THE BUDGET, THEY SAP THE SPIRIT AND DESTROY INCENTIVE. WE ALL KNOW THE JOY OF A JOB WELL DONE AND PRIDE OF PERSONAL ACHIEVEMENT. THESE GOOD FEELINGS ARE AS IMPORTANT IN THE FACTORIES AS THEY ARE IN THE EXECUTIVE SUITE. IT IS ONLY BY THE SPIRIT OF LEARNING AND DOING AND EARNING THAT NATIONAL PROSPERITY WILL PERSIST. WE HAVE OUR CHOICE; EITHER WE HAVE AN ENTERPRISE SOCIETY OR AN ENTITLEMENT SOCIETY, BUT WE CAN'T HAVE BOTH.

1993

...It's easy for you to say...but, I just lost my job...

One of the "most asked questions" to us is what is happening in our economy where thousands of people are being laid off. What really are we going through?

Scott Burns, in a recent article in *The Dallas Morning News*, gave us some excellent reporting for a change. (Scott is an excellent journalist and we have great respect for his reporting ability. However, sometimes his viewpoint isn't exactly ours, but what else is new?)

Most people who lose their job, in retrospect, realize it wasn't all caused by the economy. Eventually they see it was the mistake of not continuing their important educational endeavor. Quick study and learning, in the end, years are left behind.

The table on the next page shows employment trends, both today and "yesterday." Carefully review the data below. While the numbers are "out-of-date," winter 2013, you should be able to see the point."

Michael Cox, a Federal Reserve economist, says that many people feel bad about the economy and that very few are optimistic. One answer, according to Mr. Cox, is that they have the wrong approach.

At A Glance Employment Trends		
Jobs Destroyed	**Today**	**Yesterday**
Railroad workers	231,000	2.1 million***
Farm workers	851,000	11.5 million**
Blacksmiths	nominal	238,000**
Watchmakers	nominal	101,000***
Harness makers	nominal	109,000***
Jobs Created	**Today**	**Yesterday**
Truck, Bus, cab driver	3.3 million	0*
Pilots and mechanics	232,000	0*
Engineers	1.8 million	38,000*
Computer programmers	1.3 million	nominal****
Fax machine workers	699,000	nominal****
*1900 **1910 ***1920 ****1960		
SOURCE: Michael Cox, Federal Reserve Bank of Dallas		

Growth is the wrong metaphor, that's not the way it works. **Economies don't grow, they evolve. The economy recreates itself.**

Mr. Cox goes on to say that this "growth" concept is wrong and that in looking at pure growth, we assume that economies are fixed in form and don't change except to get bigger. One of the outstanding truths is that we are evolving from the Industrial or Smokestack Age to the Information Age.

As one set of jobs is destroyed by change, Mr. Cox says, another set of jobs is created. More important: "You can't save jobs. ...and if you try you will reduce the capacity of the economy to adapt and change." We are in a paradigm shift. We are between what our parents knew, and what the economy will be.

In the past, jobs lasted a generation. It was common for the young to apprentice and to learn a trade. Sometimes that trade was passed on from father to son.

In our own research, we have discovered that children today can expect four jobs in their lifetimes, three of which haven't been invented yet.

So what is the answer? Most of us define ourselves by what we do— our occupations. So if we are to move into this information Age, the reality of accelerating change requires us to constantly work at preparing ourselves for new vocations; and value ourselves for our capacity to learn and adapt and not for a particular job.

Both tasks are easier said than done.

February 1994

The Penalty of In and Out Investing…

In a recent quantitative analysis of investor behavior conducted by the DALBAR Financial Services, Inc. we found some interesting statistics passed on to us by the Pasadena Group of mutual funds in their most recent quarterly bulletin.

From 1983 through 1993, the S&P 500 Stock Index with dividends reinvested returned 293 percent. During this same period the returns of surveyed equity mutual fund investors showed only 70 percent to 90 percent gains. Why? While many fund managers failed to "beat the market", this was not the correct answer. According to DALBAR the answer was poor market timing on the part of investors. Money cannot grow unless it stays invested for the entire period. **Investment return appears to be far more dependent on investor behavior than fund performance.**

June 1994

We mentioned in the last issue of FACTS that DALBAR Financial Services, a leading consulting firm for banks, insurers, fund managers, etc., had recently run a fairly comprehensive survey among mutual fund investors. This survey, which began in 1984, covered a statistically significant group of investors. I might remind you that "B" shares or back end loaded funds (with penalty for withdrawals in the first five years) were relatively unknown at that time. In addition, the sales charges in "load funds" were typically much higher than they are now.

Observation – Current

Nothing's changed. Market timing will not work on a consistent basis. Mr. Market will trick you into thinking you've "broken the code"—About the time you're counting your profits, the next rebound starts and...it's called WHIPSAW!

To review – DALBAR

Equity /growth buyers of load funds did 22.2% better than their no load counterparts (90.2% + for the load funds, and just 70.2% + for the advertised direct marketed funds).

Fixed income funds have substantially the same record: 94.7%+ for the sales charge funds, and only 77.2% + for the mail order variety.

Now folks buy no load funds to save the sales charge. The concept is simple enough: get 100% of your money to work immediately; not just 92% or 96%, the whole 100% and you are bound to win. Right? Wrong! *Even with good managers, the money must stay invested. It's impossible to move it in and out and get the same results.*

The above numbers prove it. The folks who hire the postal person to be their investment conduit or rely on the oft times mired 800 number are clearly likely to panic over every headline or pay close attention to some dunce on CNBC busily selling his or her wares to the detriment of sound investment logic.

WHILE WE WOULD LIKE TO BE THE GURU THAT YOU THINK WE ARE, THE PLAN IS SIMPLE: HIRE GREAT MANAGERS AND FIRE POOR ONES; THINK LONG RATHER THAN SHORT TERM; ADD TO EQUITY AND GROWTH ACCOUNTS WHEN THE MARKETS ARE IN TURMOIL AND PRICES ARE CHEAP; BET ON THE LONG TERM SECULAR GROWTH OF AMERICA AND THE FREE WORLD OR PERHAPS TODAY THE WHOLE WORLD; AND BE PATIENT AND CONSISTENT. HOW CAN YOU LOSE?

Un-helped and unschooled investors typically chase "up markets" and jump ship in the downturn. DALBAR adds, "While investors of all types of funds have missed the boat, "no load" fund investors tended to react more aggressively to extreme market movements." During the month of Black Monday, October 1987, no load folks were net liquidators to the tune of 7.55% of assets, while broker assisted clients, more disciplined with help, tipped the scales with only 1.87% net withdrawals.

Fixed income funds (those are the bond funds Aunt Suzy bought at the bank because she was told they were guaranteed by the federal government) were even worse; mail order liquidations were 10% while load funds in the same category posted a gain of 1.2 percent!

It is interesting. No one advocates no load law…or no load medicine or mail order dentistry. The reasons are clear enough. Yes, you can defend yourself in court, and likely lose, and yes, you can rely on aspirin for every malady, and likely just get sicker… Same for cavities, and all manner of professional services, from a plumber to the electrician.

But such is life: "As long as the lunch is free, it's bound to be good."

As our X-Generation kids would say, "NOT."

January1995

So What Makes You So Confident? It Looks Like The Sky Is Falling To Me

To back up my faith in the future, let's look at the past. *Forbes* magazine In their December 19, 1994 issue, gave us some excellent information in John Rutledge's column. He suggests that we look behind the numbers at the reality of our lives. Life expectancy at birth has increased from 70.8 years in 1970 to 75.4 years in 1990. The average work week is down from 37.1 hours in 1970 to 34.5 hours in 1990, and get this...annual paid vacation days are up from 15.5 to 22.5, meaning theoretically at least, we have more leisure time to spend.

In addition, there are twice as many boats, eight times as many RVs, six times as many adult softball teams, and sixteen million more golfers than there were in 1970. The average new home grew from 1500 to 2080 square feet. This is in addition to microwave ovens, fax machines, cellular phones, laser printers, answering machines, radial tires, CDs and video games. Rutledge believes the quality of our lives is so good that few of us would want to be exiled to the 1970s for life.

And I say, "amen."

October 1995

Where are "The Poor Folks...?"

Where did all those former middle-class people go? Well, they didn't join the ranks of the poor. Instead, Just as the American economy pulled its most talented people out of poverty in the 50s, it pulled the ablest of its middle class into the affluence of the 1980s. Government had little to do with it.

As recently as 1967, only slightly more than 1 million American families earned more than $100,000 a year. By 1980, 2.7 million households had incomes of $100,000 or more. By 1993, this group had doubled again to 5.6 million. Today almost 1 million American households have incomes over $200,000. **"Why 100 is down— They've moved up!"**

And America's wealth is not concentrated in the hands of an elite caste. The top 1% of income earners is not getting rich by itself. On the contrary, new money is finding its way to a population that is not only rapidly growing but also heterogeneous. In the entrepreneurial wealth creation world, gender and skin color have no enemies. **"This has really spread wealth."**

"This is the way it's done!"

Journalists and populist politicians have always shot arrows at the upper income groups. Those people who have put in the sixteen and eighteen hour days during the 80's and have profited by hard work (and a lot of good luck!) were targets during the 1992 presidential elections. They responded with authority at the ballot box in November of 1994.

"So where do we fit in...?"

As more and more American corporations "downsize" and as middle management baby-boomers by necessity become entrepreneurs, they are discovering the realities of making payrolls while at the same time financing government bureaucracies. You'll see not only more and more families moving into the upper income brackets, but you'll see a demand from these very same people that government downsize its operations. With politicians having a propensity to attempt to divide our country into classes (blacks against whites, what appears to be a catastrophic browns against blacks, rich against poor, etc.) a whole new democracy will emerge from society. Where we end up is anybody's guess, but one thing is for sure, those of us who quit learning and refuse to move into the

Information Age, will certainly be in a class all by ourselves…**and it won't be the upper one**.

"Worried? Forget it…"

Perhaps you're worried about inflation or recession or falling profits, or even that the Democrats will sweep the White House and Congress and raise taxes which just might spook investors.

Now let's assume that you are a buy-and-hold investor (all of ours are) and you know that the worst time to sell is when the market is falling.

Our answer: ignore big worries about the market. Hold. Don't sell. Maybe even buy.

Sanford C. Bernstein and Co., the research and money management firm, says, "Stock gains tend to come in brief, intense bursts. Miss enough of them and you lose all the advantage of stock investing in the first place."

Since 1962, stocks have returned 1% per month on an average. During the best 60 months in those 70 years, the average stock return was 12% (per month!) In all of the other months—that is, 93% of the time, stocks returned close to 0. If you missed those bursts—those intense moments when the stock market stops vacillating up and down from one day to the next, and makes this dramatic progress, you've missed growth. The problem is, it's virtually impossible for anyone to predict when that will happen. **"Don't even think it'll work—Because it won't…"**

Now if you could anticipate bear markets and get out at the right time, then back in at the bottom, you'd increase your returns tremendously. If… When I hear that, I think of our old friend Don Meredith's saying: "If *ifs* and *buts* were candy and nuts, we'd all have a Merry Christmas." No way, Jay! We've found out the hard way that market timers, sooner or later, end up like old-time gun-fighters: dead.

September and the anticipation of crisp fall days always inspires me to talk about stock markets,

It turned out that July was roller coaster time for stock mutual funds. The Investment Company Institute reported that a record number of dollars fled those funds during the hot month. (As a point of interest, we at Omega set a record for investing in July.) In retrospect when you look at the market comeback of August and early September, the flight from the funds was a knee-jerk reaction, mostly having to do with emotional people who use no-help funds (Sorry, should be no-load). And many of these investors are paying a 1% fee to their advisors to tell them when to be "in" and when to be "out."

"Go play golf and forget it…"

While our investors do not seem to be as concerned as most, I have observed that the general public is quite concerned with what the markets are going to do next. This is unfortunate since it's impossible to know what markets are going to do next. And, the fact of the matter is, it really doesn't matter what the "Market" is going to do next. I can assure you that over the next six months it will not be the same as it is today. It'll be either higher or lower. (How's that for a forecast?!)

A wise lady who writes for the Dow Jones Investment Advisor, has an interesting comment about this: "I haven't the foggiest notion, whether on its way to 50,000, the Dow Jones will stop at 4,500 or 6,500 next. Don't know. Can't know. Don't care. Doesn't matter. Over and Out…" And we might add: the losses have always been temporary, the gains always permanent.

What does it matter about the market? It is time and energy wasted worrying about it. It's unknowable.

May 1987

"Hey cousin…be sure to hold your nose…"

In a recent speech by Dan Sullivan, he tells of a friend of his who was watching cliff diving in Acapulco on television. The camera all of a sudden panned up on the next diver and it turned out to be the viewer's cousin. He was stunned. His cousin was a trained diver who had competed in college, but this was a different situation! So he watched his cousin dive and it was a successful one. He saw him about four weeks later and he said, "Gee, I was flabbergasted to see you dive from so high."

His cousin says, "Well, you know, it is not the distance that gets you." But in Acapulco there is a bit of a trick—you have to catch the surf when you dive. So you have to dive when you see the rocks.

"If you dive when you see the water, what you get are rocks."

Is this truth transferrable when it comes to investing?

April 1997

Memories… Memories… Memories…

We here at Omega keep a series of clippings taken from *The Wall Street Journal* during adverse market times: We call it our "scrap book." Over the last couple of years we have not added to our scrapbook. There has been no drastically down-turning market since July of 1994. However, that has changed with the multi-point drop of the Dow Jones Industrial average during the last few days. You see, when prices drop drastically in one or two days people begin to bail out of various segments of the market. One of our favorite scrap book items is the story that appeared in *The Wall Street Journal* in the fall of 1994 that announced mass liquation of bond funds. Literally billions of dollars flowed from bond funds as interest rates moved upward. During that period of time we here at Omega began to invest many of our client's monies into income, bond-laden mutual funds, and needless to say that has paid off handsomely for our clients, since shortly stock markets stabilized and (sure enough!) interest rates turned downward.

August 1998

Mutterings From the Battlefield…

A new book by Harry S. Dent, Jr., an economist/futurist, entitled The Roaring 2000s contains a vision of a boom-time ahead. He compares the period of years from 1998 to 2009 to the "Roaring Twenties." He cites the growing power of the Baby Boomers and the technological revolution of the Internet being the components that will bring about major economic changes.

Mr. Dent believes that the suburbs will grow crowded in the first decade of the 21st century, and as more Baby Boomers age and the availability of telecommuting technology increases, people will move to small towns, resort areas, and exurbs (the area surrounding suburbs). Other futurists maintain that the $395,000 house your neighbor just bought in the suburbs will not be appealing to the new, younger generation coming along, and there will be more sellers than buyers for residential real estate. **"Ever met a market Guru who was always right?"**

"When experts talk, be sure to add a grain of salt."

Dent's advice in regard to investment strategies is to ride the current boom with stocks until 2006 or 2008. The next step he suggests is to move into bonds and treasury bills. Around 2010, after a correction, he predicts most of your money should go into foreign securities and… well, I'll save the rest for your guesses…. Rick Wilson, an Arlington, Texas, economist and outspoken commentator, singled out a quote in a recent newsletter from The Wall Street Journal on June 26, 1998: "Experts advise steering clear of Asian stocks." Rick says that when the experts begin to say avoid, nine times out of ten it is a time to buy… His stock market forecast? In a word—up—but not without the volatility we're experiencing today… Our friend Robert Vrees, in his *Executive Reviews*, points out that *Money Magazine's* August issue says that David Alger (Alger Funds) runs five mutual funds, four variable annuity accounts, four portfolios that are sold to 401(k) plan sponsors, and seventy private accounts sold to wealthy individuals and pension funds. Money says that when you have a hot or popular manager, you should leverage the name as far as it will go… Jean-Marie Eveillard, the great SoGen International fund manager, is now managing three funds and two annuity accounts. Helen Young Hayes manages about $21 billion in mutual funds and 10 annuity accounts for Janus. We wonder from this standpoint how long it will take the public to figure out that the funds that these people manage must be watched closely because burn-out is burn-out… James O'Shaughnessy of O'Shaughnessy Capital Management says he has been a bear since 1994 but has been 100% in stocks since then as well. Why? Simple math. Stocks have gone up 71% of the time since the opening of the New York Stock Exchange. No matter what you think is going to happen, the trend is positive."

Long-term views and rear view mirrors

Several fundamental trends support the long-term outlook for a positive economic environment. For example, there is a great need for the Baby Boomers to save more for retirement and an even greater need for saving to rise in the rest of the developed world (with much of it likely to flow into U.S. markets). We see a generally positive political environment if for no other reason the dawning of the information age. We commented recently that if CNN had been available in the 30s, Hitler would probably have never come to power, especially with Mr. Roosevelt as President.

A number of economists have also looked at our environment and pondered whether an era of permanent prosperity with mild decelerations in growth will be as bad as it gets. For decades, economists thought that somehow economic upturns not only did but also should last about three years. Imbalances of some sort were seemingly inevitable, and the party was over when these demons arrived at the door. In those days business people groped in the dark without computerized record keeping to figure out production schedules and inventories and economists were only tiptoeing into the microchip generation.

Obviously, there are problems in predicting permanent prosperity. The last time anyone thought economists and brilliant government officials might have the business cycle licked was in the 1960s. What followed was the economic nightmare of the 1970s. One thing that we probably know is that there is no chance that our monetary policy will go back to the stop-and-go pattern of the early post-World War II period. Another thing that we know is that we'll never go back to the rotary dial telephone. In the Industrial Age our natural resources were finite: oil, land, water, etc. In the computerized Information Age where knowledge is the major resource, proliferation of that resource is relatively easy.

September 1995

Quote of the Month

> *"From 1953 to 1984, a period of 31 years, the stock market went up 935 points... On Mondays, it went down 1,565. So on non-Mondays, it was up 2,500 points. It wasn't a coincidence that the big decline in 1987, last October, and this week was on a Monday. People on the weekend become economists. They become portfolio strategists. But they don't look at their portfolios; they're reading the newspapers. They're responding to all these scary stories. After that, they're bold if they take their lunch to work on Monday."*

> — Peter Lynch
> Former manager of Fidelity Magellan Fund
> *The New York Times*, September 06, 1998

"Share your brains please!"

Poor Butterfly... er, People

A recent issue of *The Wall Street Journal* gave us some very interesting statistics gleaned from a Census Bureau release on income and poverty in the United States. The report indicates that 30 million Americans are living in poverty. Poverty does not suggest destitution—the inability to provide a family with adequate food, clothing, and shelter. While that's what most of us think poverty is, it doesn't quite hold true when you've seen some statistics drawn from Federal government reports.

"Poor Butterfly..."

- In 1995, 41% of all "poor" households own their own homes—3 bedrooms, 1½ baths, a garage, and a porch or patio.

- Over 750,000 more "poor" people own homes valued at more than $150,000; nearly 200,000 own homes worth more than $300,000.

- The average poor American has one-third more living space than the average Japanese and four times more living space than the average Russian – that's the average citizen in Japan or Russia, not the average poor person.

- 70% of poor households own a car; 27% own two or more cars.

And, here's one: poor children actually consume more meat than higher income children and have higher average protein intakes—100% above recommended levels. On an average, they are one inch taller and ten pounds heavier than the GIs that stormed the beach of Normandy in 1944. As you might suspect, the Census Bureau and their poverty report is simply inaccurate.

According to *The Wall Street Journal*, "For decades both conventional wisdom and the census bureau have told us that 'the rich get richer and the poor get poorer.' This is untrue. The material conditions of lower income Americans have improved dramatically over time."

April 1999

"Have they made a movie of it yet?"

If you haven't read Tom Brokaw's recent book on the World War II generation, *The Greatest Generation*, you owe it to yourself to at least read a review. The group of people that he writes about grew up during the depression, saved the world from tyranny, and engineered America's greatest economic expansion which provided sound footing on which democracy and capitalism spread throughout the world. Brokaw writes about many individuals who have amassed more wealth than they ever dreamed of. What's amazing in his book is that in talking to these folks most of them don't think they did anything particularly special.

Evan Siminoff of *Financial Planning* magazine points out the difference in the feats these people accomplished and the meager achievements of the Baby Boom Generation. "The gap is pathetic!", Siminoff notes. "I'm always embarrassed when I hear boomers tout their own generation's accomplishments." The easiest explanation is that, to some extent, we are all accidents of history.

Mr. Siminoff goes on to say that it appears parenting was the generation's biggest failure, guilty of only wishing that their children could have everything they never had. An understandable parental aspiration, no doubt, but the result was that the Bob Doles of the world raised the Bill Clintons. Siminoff continues by saying, "Still, if high hopes and generosity are a person's greatest fault they are marks of personal character." **"Mr. Siminoff, please go over that one more time."**

January 2000

Just Another Illusion

Gazoots! I know you thought miracles had ceased with bible days, but finally another one has been reported. Joe Hardgrove agrees with syndicated columnist Jane Bryant Quinn.

We spoke in our last newsletter about the repeal of the Glass-Stegall Act whereby banks, brokerage firms, and insurance companies will be allowed to merge. Ms. Quinn tackles the same subject in a recent column.

Now don't get me wrong, I'm all for deregulation. For example, when the government finally deregulated the airlines, ticket prices for vacationers and everyone else plunged. And now we get great service. Yeah right! Although the savings and loan shenanigans cost taxpayers billions, bank savers started earning higher real returns on their deposits in the 80's. As time goes by we'd hope that expenses and fees on financial products would be reduced because of competition. But combining brokerage firms, banks, and insurance companies is not our idea of competition. The Internet has made consumers shoppers. They shop product by product in a fiercely competitive national market. And it's clear that as an investor's assets increase, she has a tendency to unbundle her relationships. She looks for the best deal from a number of financial service providers.

But back to our agreement with Ms. Quinn regarding mergers of these major financial institutions: She points out that you can forget privacy. And as we stated in our last *Opinions & Facts*, it's trade time when it comes to your name and phone number between the insurance, brokerage, credit card companies, and Lord knows who else. Ditto your medical records; and what about life insurance sales solicitation? Recent class action lawsuits certainly have thrown the spotlight on many bad sales practices by some of the oldest insurance companies in the country. Anybody ever buy a life insurance policy thinking it was an "investment account?"

Hey, here's a pretty good idea. Buy a CD from your friendly mega bank then buy life insurance and let the interest from the CD pay the premium.

"Don't Try This Without a Seatbelt...!"

The problem you ask...Well, it just might be the interest rate will go down and the return on your CD won't be enough to pay the premium. But don't worry, because you can always make a bank loan to take care of that. And on...and on....

One of the major pitfalls here is that we don't know who is in charge of oversight.

Will the Securities and Exchange Commission and the NASD govern the brokerage firms that the insurance companies own? Or will it be the banking regulators, or maybe the State Insurance Commissioner who oversees the insurance company... Which owns a bank?

If you think this is confusing, just wait until you try to get your mutual fund balance from the computer at your megabank, owned by an insurance company.

No matter whose turf is stepped on, the squeals will be loud and long from the bureaucracy.

Only time will tell how this whole thing will work out. But one thing we believe: the service will not improve and the costs will certainly not come down."

February 2000

"My own private take..." —Joe Hardgrove

The seasons turn and all the rivers flow into the sea. The Forever Things are inevitable. We reflect on the manias of the past and know the ending. Yet the intensity and excitement of this phenomenon will never be short of over expectant participants.

Memories are extremely short, especially in the area of newly arrived investors and their investment advisors. More information on investing is available today than any time in history; however, it seems to me that wisdom is in short supply. No matter what CNN and CNBC tells you, trees do not grow to the sky.

Recently, I had an opportunity to catch up on some of my reading from *The New York Times* book review. Adam Smith, author of *The Money Game*, *Super Money*, and *Paper Money*, reviewed an interesting book by Edward Chancellor. It is called *Devil Take the Hind Most—A History of Financial Speculation*.

"Why-oh-why didn't I start with *The Great Gatsby*?"

Why I decided to catch up on this particular article I don't know. And quite frankly, after I began to read the review, I wondered why I didn't start up with something more fun. Chancellor, who is a free lance contributor to the *Financial Times of London* and an economist, writes a book that covers a number of speculative fevers. The South Sea Bubble of 1720, Enthusiasm for Emerging Markets in the London of 1820; and the British Railway of the '40s, are only a few tales. Chancellor even covers the shenanigans of Michael Milken and Ivan Boesky, Junk Bond Kings, whom it seems were around just a few weeks ago.

"Come fly with me!"

And speaking of excesses, in the 1980s he reminds us that Susan Gutfreud, wife of the CEO of Solomon Brothers, spent $20 million redecorating her apartment and booking two seats on the Concord to fly a cake to her husband's birthday party in Paris. And just think, this was before dot-com IPO's.

"Joe, you've turned negative!"

Don't think I'm suddenly looking at the glass as half empty, because mine is always half full. However, when I read Chancellor's story of the Japanese real estate and stock market boom of the '80s, I begin to shiver just a little. The boom in Japan, which many believe the Japanese government started, was known as *Baburu*, the bubble economy. Japanese companies engaged in Zeitach-financial engineering speculation—and the stock market profits of Matsushita, Toyota, and Nissan and Sharp, were greater than their operating profits from television sets and cars. The Tokyo Dow Jones went up ten times and housewives visited their brokers daily. Successful speculators were known as *Shinjinrui*—"New People"—as opposed to "working people." Chancellor reminds us that during the late '80s the Baburu grew and grew as Americans fretted that Japan was becoming number one. At the peak the grounds of the Imperial Palace in Tokyo were estimated to have a greater value than all of California. This is something that sounds familiar these days: the bank of Japan was afraid that this frenzy might end in a crash so they gently increased interest rates. As we all know, expensive credit is a bubble killer. Chancellor points out that there was no crash, but the Japanese market floated down 60% and scarcely recovered after 8 years.

"So how does this relate to me?"

Well, so be it. We go on and on watching our neighbors inflate their portfolios with over priced tech stocks and mutual funds while we try to keep our sanity and stay balanced. "I've got to catch up," they say. "Fifteen percent just isn't enough."

"Get rid of that fund, it's been down for the last 27 minutes."

It's a hard trip, folks. If you don't believe me you should eyeball the people who call and want to liquidate their dividend paying blue chip domestic funds, as the market gives a billion-dollar value to a two-year-old company losing money.

June 2000

"Risk takers listen up."

In 1999 the markets for stocks ended on a strong note. Investors were continually rewarded for taking as much risk as possible throughout the year, but especially during the fourth quarter. Risk taking by investors carried over into the year 2000 and more and more money went into the most aggressive funds. Thus the axiom that momentum investing is the way to go led the unsuspecting to this trap during the first two months of this year. Speculative excesses in technology areas in late February was attributed to "buying without regard to price." No matter how you look at it, future earnings have to be considered in making the decision to buy or sell a stock. It is our belief after more than three decades in this business that the only way to win, over the long haul, is to have consistent long-term professional management."

Is stock picking back in vogue? How big can the bubble get?

A recent article in *Business Week* points out that valuations investors have put on Internet companies would require a repeal of some basic tenants of investing. As we all need to remember, the worth of an enterprise must reflect its earnings capacity. Today's investors, however, are investing for even higher share prices rather than dividends or growth in corporate value. The flight from *Old Economy* blue chips to tech stocks, then from Internet retailers to business-to-business companies, then back to blue chips is classic herd mentality. The interesting thing about this trend today is the market valuations on Internet stocks are predicated on unreal profit margins which only a small percentage of those companies have. When this bubble bursts it probably will take a number of the other stocks down.

Now here's where we come in. When these stocks go on sale and have reasonable valuation, historically this is the time that nobody wants to buy. Remember, the public always buys high and sells low. But people who have done proper research i.e., professional managers and stock analysts, know better than the day-trader when the right time to buy occurs. However it's amazing to see the number of people who really believe they can manage their money without research.

April 2001

"But this is not easy!"

It's a tough thing to continue investing when the fund you are buying is going down on a weekly basis. This is the ideal way to do it and it's been proven over the years that it works better this way than just the opposite. The toughest thing to do is to buy when things are down in price. Most people think they'll wait until the market hits bottom. But, as the pros say, "Nobody rings a bell at the bottom." Unfortunately many investors tend to be shaken by bad experience and often make unwise decisions based on emotion. A record of $13 billion dollars flowed out of mutual funds on January 2, 2001 after the seventh worst decline in NASDAQ history. Two days later a record $17 billion flowed into mutual funds following the biggest one-day rally ever by the NASDAQ. The net result: NASDAQ up 14% in two days. Investors lose 7% as emotions overrule reason. Events like this offer compelling reasons why investors should stay in the market at all times.

September 11, 2001

Hold Fast

After the terrible tragedy that struck not only New York and Washington, but our entire Nation, and after observing how people have looked for answers, I might refer you to the Father of Solomon, the wisest man who ever lived. I hope King David's advice is considered encouragement.

> *"Do not fret because of evil men...for like the grass they will soon whither, like green plants they will soon die away. Trust in the Lord and do good...Delight yourself in the Lord...Commit your way to the Lord...Be still before the Lord and wait patiently for Him; do not fret when men succeed in their ways when they carry*

out their wicked schemes...Refrain from anger and turn from wrath; do not fret, it leads only to evil."

— The 37th Psalm, a song of David.

Other voices make sense

Our friend Byron Green, at Green Investment Management, has some interesting comments following the tragedy in New York and Washington. He points out that when it's all over, economic fundamentals will drive stock prices. This particular tragedy came when the U. S. had been struggling to find a bottom to the current economic slow down. Byron continues, "We look for authorities in both banking and political systems to be prepared to do whatever is required to assure that economic stability is maintained." He also notes that essential banking operations have not been disrupted.

...and we think...

We expect the markets to open after the weekend (this is being written on 9/13/2001) and the Federal Reserve will probably act aggressively in reducing interest rates and probably international interest rates will also be lowered.

"This is Tough Stuff!"

January 2002

To Index or Not to Index

The implosion of Enron stock, once the shining star of the Standard and Poor 500 Stock Index, brings to a climax our beliefs that the thought of buying a mutual fund that mirrors the S&P is as dead as a Palestinian suicide bomber.

During the Bull Market of the '90s, John Bogle, developer of Index funds and head of The Vanguard Group, convinced journalists and investors alike that his Vanguard 500 Index fund would fit all comers. As early as mid-summer of 2001, he continued to tell us that no one should be without the magic of Indexing.

Not to be outdone, Jonathan Clements, columnist at *The Wall Street Journal*, as late as July 15, 2001, was still saying that the only way a manager can beat the Index is to be lucky. "But who wants to rely on luck," Clements continues, "Especially when there is a sure fire alternative. That alternative is market tracking Index Funds." We beg to differ.

"Tell us why"

First, you must remember who develops the portfolio for the S&P Index Fund. It's not the money managers, it's executives at Standard and Poor Corporation. People who establish those Indexes base their decisions on the capitalized valuation of the considered companies. In other words, highest market valued stocks receive the highest weightings in the fund. Thus, instead of being invested equally into each of 500 stocks, the index fund investor has his money not really diversified, but more loaded to the "hottest" growth entities in that Index. This explains why so many baths were taken in the Enron debacle and why highly capitalized technology stocks were added to the 500 during the roaring market of the '90s. When the bubble burst, the mutual funds out there in the marketplace that had excellent experienced managers picking reasonably valued stocks firmly out performed those Indexes during the flat and down market periods.

"OK, John what do you think about your invention?"

In a summertime article by Charles Jaffey, a *Boston Globe* columnist, there appeared a very interesting interview with Mr. Bogle. As an acquaintance of Mr. Bogle for a number of years, I can tell you that, although he's retired, he remains a dynamic and driven individual. No matter that he's had a heart transplant!

He does give us some great ideas in regard to a number of things, among them: we should look for low expenses when buying funds. He says, "a 1% or 2% difference in return per year over a lifetime of 8% rather than 10%, …and you are talking about giving up 30% of the market's cumulative compounded return over time. That's an enormous sacrifice though it seems small when you make it." This of course, is the difference between the average cost of investment management 1% to 2% (that's $100 to $200 per year for every $10,000 under management) and as an example, 0.7%, which is what most of our funds charge.

But Mr. Bogle goes on to say in Jaffey's column in regard to indexing: "I have to take some responsibility for what's happening, and I don't like it much."

"Says Bogle"
"Indexing simply doesn't work as well as I would have hoped and they don't work as well, not because Indexing is a problem but because the Indexes are a problem. There is too much turnover. As a result, I'm a bit troubled by my creation like Dr. Frankenstein. It's not that growth and value Indexing or Small Cap Indexing haven't worked for investors, but they just aren't a clear cut success as Total Market Indexing."

Looks like Mr. Bogle still hasn't gotten off the dead horse.

"John, you're not all wrong."
However, he does give us a forward looking prediction. "Over the next decade we're not going to see much more than 8, 9 or maybe 10% returns." Mr. Bogle, along with this writer, believes that the thing we should all do is to lower our expectations for the future. It's pretty difficult to believe that we're going to get the 15–20% return over the next decade that we got over the last ten years.

A case in point
Recently a client of ours, who sits on the board of a major non-profit organization, informed us that that organization's endowed portfolio had lost in excess of 30% from September of 1999 to September of 2001. We ran a hypothetical illustration using the identical funds that were in our client's account over the same period

and showed an increase in the account. We suggested that she show the results to the people in the organization who make those investment decisions.

When asked later where the investment people had decided to place what was left of the money she said, "Index Funds."

Index Funds may not be the buggy whip and dinosaur of the next decade, but we believe it'll be quite a while before throwing money at an unmanaged index will make an investor rich.

"Tell me how I can compare mine with the Market"

If you would like the guide on how your fund does opposed to the S&P 500 Vanguard Index, simply check the Vanguard Total Market Index and Vanguard 500's record in the newspaper and compare it to the results over one year, three years or five years compared to your funds. I think you'll see that you are better off relying on experienced managers buying stocks of well researched companies than going gangbusters in the bull market years and then being disseminated when things turn.

Spring 2002

"Who has my money?"

We at Omega have long chanted in our on-going mantra the importance of having well trained, long tenured, bright and courageous money managers in charge of client assets. You don't simply go to an Ivy League school, get a Harvard Degree, and become a successful money manager. On the contrary, when you do it and do it right, it's almost a boring chore, unless of course, you're with a fund company that chooses to anoint you as one of their "Stars." The problem with "Stars" is that many of them fall, especially when markets become complicated, flat or bearish. Those are the days when, as Mr. Warren Buffet puts it, "the tide goes out and you see who's swimming naked."

Based on the latest available data, the average fund manager in the marketplace today has a tenure of 3.7 years. Most of us have suits that old that are still in style.

One of the tasks here at Omega is to keep track of who's managing money and what moves are being made with managers. Over the last twelve to fourteen months managers of mutual funds have had a tendency to float and move. We've read where some have gone into the advertising and fashion design business!

Why we/you aren't affected

You should be aware that Omega has followed the same tried and true pattern in searching out money managers for decades. We first look for those managers with long tenure. The average time spent managing money by the people that we've utilized is in excess of twenty years. These managers are shareholders in their management company and are well paid. We insist on low annual expenses, low portfolio turnover and below average risk taking.

So with the exodus of many of the young Wall Street stars, we prefer to put our clients' money with people who do boring research and analysts who actually meet with company executives and visit the workforce in the trenches. Many have graduate degrees in the industries in which they are specializing, are bi-lingual and have the courage not to buy when the balance sheet says "No."

Summer 2003

Ideas and Comments… Hopefully Accurate… While wondering whatever happened to Jack Dreyfus…

In case you haven't kept up, President Bush has signed a tax bill which features, among other things, a lowering of tax brackets, and dividend and capital gain tax reductions. On dividends, the tax is 15% rather than the 38.5% top bracket. Long term capital gain taxes will drop from 20% to 15%.…

"And Then There's Retirement"

Companies are now increasingly moving away from traditional, fully-funded pensions to other type retirement plans such as 401(k)s. The guaranteed pensions that employees have banked on for so many years are mostly under funded. In order to fund them the company must make cash infusions into those plans and in some cases the current economic climate is forcing a number of firms into bankruptcy, which ends the guaranteed pension that people had planned on... Companies all across the country are considering cutting back or limiting pension benefits and contributions to 401(k) plans. However, those companies who are able to keep their plans going are given wide leeway by the IRS to make higher contributions by the employees and the companies...

Most experts agree that mutual funds must cut the cost of management and distribution if they are to survive. Many equity funds have expense ratios of more than 1.5% per year. After adjusting to these expenses the average equity mutual fund underperformed its appropriate comparison index.... Fortunately the majority of the funds we have under supervision charge less than half that figure, around 0.7% expense ratio.... While many critics have pointed fingers and thrown rocks at the mutual fund industry, we have observed since the late '50s that mutual funds have always been great investments for individual investors. Mutual funds have provided a low cost effective way for individuals to invest in diversified portfolios of stocks or bonds, domestic or international....

The existence of mutual funds has also helped the great expansion of the 401(k) plan—the key vehicle through which millions of American workers are accumulating money for their retirement... and without mutual funds, 401(k) participants would have far fewer choices for investments.... Professional management at lower cost has benefited Americans since the thirties...one out of five stocks lost 60% or more during the recent bear market while one out of 807 mutual funds lost 60% or more during that period of time....

Polls are very interesting. In a recent poll of U.S. residents regarding the wealth level of this country, 19% of the people polled said they were in the top 1% of wealthy Americans, 20% said they would be there soon…think about it…The fact is that the number of people with financial assets of at least $1 million actually declined last year…. This report from Cap Gemini Ernst & Young and Merrill Lynch, concluded that there were two million wealthy people in the country at the end of 2002, down from 2.1 million the previous year… *The NY Times* further reports that the number of wealthy people worldwide grew to 7.3 million from 7.1 million the year before.…

> *"There are only two people that can sabotage your portfolio: You and/or your portfolio advisor."*

SECTION II

Memories and Letters
To Clients

This is a section which gives some sample periodic letters we've written to our clients. Most of them are attached to monthly or quarterly investment reports. In almost every letter we attempt to give some positive advice to our clients and also chose to continue our "marketing efforts" even after the clients have come aboard. As you can see, we do this by repeating statements we've made in our original *Opinions & Facts* and letters. These writings have not been edited or approved by any governmental or self regulatory organization in the United States. They represent strictly our independent beliefs and thoughts.

June 2010

A number of our clients have called recently pretty much on edge because of the volatility of the "stock market." They have become concerned following the near 80% increase in the market since March 9, 2009. Eying these sudden downturns, blood pressures rose with the negative words coming from the talking heads on CNBC and the 1000 point drop in the Dow Jones Industrial, almost ignoring its quick recovery on the same day. These are nerve-wracking moments and we have a couple of responses.

First, you shouldn't pay a great deal of attention to sudden drastic moves of the stock market either in the Dow Jones or the S&P 500. Out of the multitude of stocks that are in the portfolios that are being managed for you, there are only 500 of them in the S&P 500; 30 rest in the Dow Jones Industrials and a larger number forms the NASDAQ.

Interestingly enough your portfolio may contain small percentages of these stocks which stand in the "benchmark" indexes. While trends give certain signals as to what your portfolio is doing, you must remember that you do not have an Index Fund. If your money was totally invested in an S&P 500 Index fund, you would really have reason to be worried when the indexes (markets) move downward in a volatile manner. As it is, remember that the securities in your portfolio may even be foreign or emerging market stocks (or bonds). After many years in this business and numerous conversations, we've met few professionals who spend time watching the indexes or "markets." Their attention is more on the companies that they own and are researching, which may or may not be a part of the market you see represented in the index.

The recent volatility in the markets (indexes) has been telling evidence of attempted manipulation of the market by traders who are hoping to make money on a very short term basis. And Hedge Fund gurus also stand accused. The companies and the stock that your managers analyze seldom can change 2% or 5% in a single day or even in a single week. Since most of our clients are well diversified, drastic 1 and 2 day movement has little long term effect on the portfolio. In some cases portfolio volatility occurs because of a catastrophe, but we believe that most of the blue chip growth and value companies that exist out there are being run by very educated and experienced executives who are always looking ahead and spending time to make their companies viable and growing.

It's OK if you look at your portfolio every 6 months or so and check it out, but on a daily basis? You're on the wrong track. All the daily valuation of markets and the economy should be considered exactly what they are: daily evaluations, or snapshots. The funds we offer have a long term record of outperforming the "stock markets" over scores of 10 year rolling periods anyway.

Recently we had a client who confessed to being very "worried" about the "stock market." She said, "Maybe I should just turn off my television set and quit watching." This person has been a successful client of ours for well over 2 decades. My answer to her included a chuckle, "You finally figured out how successful investors make money!"

January 2007

In reviewing 2006 I would like to utilize some quotes from the December 30th *Wall Street Journal* which sums up the past year.

> "*The Dow Jones Industrial Average closed yesterday near an all time high, up 17% for the year. Long-term bond yields rose this year but still remain remarkably low… Economic growth has slowed but remains solid. And by some measures the natural market volatility is at lows not seen in a decade—the Dow, for example, is still adding to this longest stretch (910 days) without a one day decline of 2% or more since 1900.*"

Well, this kind of news and looking at your report from us leads us to come up with the old saying that many people have forgotten:

"This time it's different"

But we know it's not different. If we believe it's different and that the markets will never fall we're setting ourselves up for a fall.

When someone tells us that the old rules don't apply anymore, we tend to check our wallets. But this is not to say that nothing ever changes. With the explosion of the information age which began in the mid 1970s and after the technology boom in the late 1990s it seems that financial stability has begun to settle over the markets. We've discovered with the use of derivatives and the globalization of investing that the economy moves everything faster. Money has become marginally cheaper and more plentiful, thus the increase in the number of hedge funds and private equity funds.

To quote the journal again: "More broadly, danger always exists from abrupt government policy shifts. Two of the biggest current risks in our view, are the chance of U.S. tax increases and that the Fed may still have underestimated the inflationary pressures it let loose in 2004 and 2005 with the lowered interest rates."

But as we enter 2007 let us remember that we still have an open economic system and as free trade proliferates and entrepreneurism multiplies we believe that you'll see more stability if you look at the long-term. As you know, we have preached the "long-term" sermon for a long time. In reviewing the last 16 years of *Opinions & Facts* I have discovered that we've been telling the same story all along. Just remember, there will always be "up markets" and "down markets"; thus the down times give the professional money managers the opportunity to find bargains for the portfolios that represent your retirement and long-term savings.

We will continue to attempt to station your assets so that you can spend your time in the noble pursuit of raising your family or enjoying your retirement and know that future generations will also reap some of the results of the seeds you have sown with us.

May the best occur for you, and your life be filled with peace during this 7th year of the 21st century.

July 2011

"How do you Increase Newspaper Circulation?"
"Easy. Just Give 'em More Bad News!"

When I read today's headlines and hear TV sound bites, the local media , and from *The New York Times*, *The Wall Street Journal*, *The Washington Post*, et al., I sometimes feel that the bad news rolling on from the media could make you want to immigrate to Costa Rica, Switzerland, or maybe Waco, Texas!

Take a look at the following urgent warnings, **"Portugal's Sovereign-Debt Rating Has Been Downgraded by Moody's To Junk Status"**... **"Moody's Warns That Understated Bank Loans Pose a Threat to China's Banking System"**... **"The Dow Jones Industrial Average Lost 12.90 Points out of Their Biggest Weekly Gain in Two Years"**... **"Heart Treatment Overused"**... **"Developed Nations See a Jump in Inflation"**.... They keep coming on like an avalanche of tsunami water, but guess what? With the glut of current news crowding our airwaves and filling newspapers and magazines, people forget to look at what's happening in the "Real World"—the world we live in.

Bad news and frightening accounts of business activity become old news in two days. However, in the field of real-life business, with rising interest rates in China, inevitable Greek default, and the end of the lame Fed bond buying binge (QE2), the market was in a six week decline. And can you imagine: from peak to trough it ran barely -7% through the first week in July. Of course at the same time in "Section B" we read of *positive* corporate revenues, cash flows, earnings, dividends, stock buy-backs, and cash position activity continuing their historic surges.

When you look at it from a logical standpoint you see that the great companies in America, and the world, have ignored these bad headlines and calmly went about their business. In fact the common stocks in this country have become "cheap." According to a recent Nick Murray interactive newsletter, quality equities are cheaper than they have been since the Korean War. He states that the S&P 500 at 1,280 is selling for 8.7 times cash flow.

Higher gasoline prices, cramped consumer budgets, and high unemployment: in spite of this, Wal-Mart just announced that a $15 billion share buyback program was near completion—they bought 244 million shares for about $13 billion since last June and they've just announced *another* $15 billion round. According to Mr. Murray, the family company Walton Enterprises, just sits there and doesn't sell. It owns the same 1.7 billion shares it always has. I'd say the Walton's are eating their own grits and gravy!

How about Exxon Mobil? This stock's price is cheaper than it was when oil was $140 a barrel in 2008. It has grown it's dividend over 9% for the past 5 years, and uses it's tremendous cash flow not just to make major new discoveries like those announced in June, but to buy back 300 to 400 million shares a year. Well, it goes on and on! (Incidentally, the people managing our money have been aware of this for quite some time).

Have you analyzed your financial situation lately? We find that many of our clients after really checking their retirement plan assets are quite surprised at how short they are. We know it's not politically correct, but maybe you should invest personally rather than take unwise allocation risks in your 401(k). Oh yes, get some help from someone who really knows how the real world works.

Few folks have adequate finances to live after retirement the way they *want* to. Most however, do not have assets that will allow them to live like they did *while* they were gainfully employed.

February 11, 2009

Dear Folks:

The volatility in the market has been a headline grabber for the last several weeks. We've observed that during time of volatility people must keep their thoughts and eyes on the future. As we wrote in our last communication making a rash decision on short term movements of the stock market doesn't pay off. Most of our clients are in particular mutual funds which have consistently outperformed "the markets" over *meaningful periods*. Of course, there are no guarantees here.

Most of our long-term clients have realized that this is the time to be patient and let the money managers look for the bargains that make for great gains in turn-around times.

According to the National Bureau of Economic Research, there have been 10 recessions since the end of World War II. The average lasted approximately 10.5 months and carried the economy down slightly less than 2%. I might further point out that over the last 25 years as the economy has deepened, our monetary tools for fighting slow-downs have improved so that the time lapse between recessions has lengthened both in their duration and depth. Additionally I would remind you that since November 1982, the economy has only been in recession for 16 months out of about 300.

Economy "slow downs" and recessions historically—on average—represent a two percent contraction on an average of every six years. We believe that this seems to be a very small price to pay for an expansion of national wealth which is ongoing, and which has produced the wealthiest society that ever existed on the earth. Downturns are a part of the cycle. We welcome it, as do our experienced managers who constantly search for bargains.

While most of the recessions are main line media driven, recessions are a part and parcel of a capitalistic society and a free market economy. As I pointed out in our last newsletter, for the patient investor, the down-turning market can be quite painful.

Rodney Smith, regional Vice President for American Funds, reminded us what our old friend Graham Holloway, former President of American Fund Distributors, said in regard to the 1974 Bear market:

"We've seen this movie before and we know how it ends. But we still cried."

What movie? For you old timers, it was "Ole Yeller."

Call us if we can be of service.

August 2009

It has come to my attention that you have some assets in Cash Management Trust, the American Fund Money Market; thus I thought I might drop you a note to make some comments.

Many of our clients desire to have substantial cash, available as emergency money, which we are certainly are in agreement with. However, stock market cycles often cause investors to do the wrong thing at the wrong time. Historically, during periods when equity returns have been relatively high, investors have flocked to the market. When equity returns have been low, many investors have left. **Precisely the time when stock values are attractive.**

GETTING OUT OF THE MARKET IS EASY, GETTING BACK IN IS THE TOUGH PART.

While your money in so called "safer" short term investments such as money market funds offer protection during volatile markets, they've also generated disappointing long term returns.

- Cash has beaten stocks and bonds in only 12 of the past 77 years, according to Ibbotson Associates.
- One dollar invested from 1926 through December 31, 2002, grew to $17.48 (T- Bills), but $1,775 if invested in stocks (the S&P 500).

Historically the benefits of being invested when a bull market begins have been profound. During the first half of all the bull markets, the Dow Jones Industrial Average has averaged +43.6%. The average return in the second half of the bull markets of the Dow has averaged 16.8%.

Our almost forty years in the investment business has shown us, once again and in most cases, that people act on their emotion. We understand that and we also understand fear of losses; however, it might be wise for you consider moving some of your cash back into the American Funds.

If you'd like to discuss this, we can do it in person or on the phone. Meanwhile we look for a stronger and sustainable economy for the future.

October 2009

Despite the fact that things have become steady here at Omega and in the marketplace in general, many investors have stayed on the sidelines, and in some cases, tremendously over-weighted in cash and cash-like investments. Their question is: "How can the market continue to go up?" The following items have put many people's investing ideas on hold:

- It's very difficult for an economy to come back after tremendous deleveraging.

- How sustainable will growth be when the so called "stimulus" goes away?

- What about government debt levels? The forecast to be 70%–80% of the gross domestic product in the US, Germany and France.

- How will the US resist solving the debt burden problem through higher inflation, thereby reducing the value of all financial assets?

The list goes on and on.

Some believe that government intervention is the answer. As an example, they say that by bailing out various financial companies, especially the monetary response with the Troubled Asset Relief Program (TARP), the banks could return to loaning money sooner. There is still $570 billion of the $787 billion of fiscal stimulus waiting to be used. The housing situation has improved; and consumer confidence has increased. While unemployment is an ongoing problem, we see that over all, income has increased. Inventories are low, thus more manufacturing should increase over the near future. The government's removal of capital from American business is a tricky play; done too soon, the recession continues or gets deeper; not soon enough, politically, the administration can run into "election year problems" from the increasing growth of the economic Conservative crowd. This problem at home along with the entire Mideast situation and the attempt to completely change 16% of the economy with the pressing of the Health Care Plan through Congress is sounding the war tocsin, and the Right is responding.

"So what should I consider?"
It is our opinion investing new money in equity mutual funds that we represent should be on a careful dollar-cost-averaging basis, since as most of you know, we do not believe in "jumping

in" and then "jumping out" at the slightest hint of negative news makes sense. **WE BELIEVE THAT WHEN THE LAST SHOT IS FIRED, THE ENTREPRENEURSHIP OF THE FREE MARKET SYSTEM WILL CONTINUE TO BRING THIS ECONOMY BACK. WE ALSO BELIEVE THAT IT WILL BE MORE OF A FACTOR THAN ALL OF THE GOVERNMENT AID THAT HAS BEEN CREATED BY PRINTING PRESSES, LOANS, AND INCREASED TAXES BOTH ON BUSINESS OWNERS AND THE WORKING CLASS.**

The "New Normal" (more on this later)

Then there are those economists and experienced investors who believe that our future will be a "New Normal." This concept is based on the knowledge that the severe recession, the change in global markets, the government's involvement in our economy now more than ever, and lack of leadership from Washington in global economic matters will make a huge dent in the economy. Some believe that we will face below average growth in our economy as well as the global economy.

This tells us that we would do well to consider diversification with fixed income, dividend paying equities and patience on the part of our investors, utilizing creative managers who can visualize these changing economies.

Certainly, since 80% of the time the equity markets both globally and domestic have out-paced downturns, almost half a century of experience has shown us that the odds of pulling out of the market at the right time and then (the hardest part) going back in at the right time is a fools errand.

"Hey, Joe. What's new?" "Not a thing. It's just as it's always been."

As we have reported to you over the last several months (probably several years!) markets do something besides *go up*. Recently in a conversation with a long time successful money manager here in Fort Worth at a recent political fundraiser, I made the statement to him that things were considerably better now than they had been over the last year. He responded by saying: "Joe, Bull markets occur, then Bear markets come along; then Bull markets appear, and then once again Bear markets. It's cyclical. You and I have known that our entire careers."

I responded, **"Yes you are so right. But people always want to do the right thing at the wrong time. Everybody loves to buy when things are going up; but when markets turn downward, for some reason they'd rather wait until the prices get higher."**

Another Bear Market is coming—You can bet on it…
It always has, it always will. And following that bear market will be another bull market. As my friend, the long time money manager said, "Things are different this time… Because they're different every time. There is always some "cause" for the market to decline."

We've discovered that Bull markets are started by optimistic investors; the "cause" of Bear markets has proven to be continued pessimism. As we've said before in many of our letters, we've never met a pessimistic individual who succeeded in reaching his financial goals.

Those of you who have bought and own equity mutual funds with us—many since the early 1970s— have discovered optimism always wins, especially when you accept the 5 truths that we have so long tried to remind you of:

1. Long tenured, well trained, experienced money managers.
2. Low cost for the service and management of money.
3. Low portfolio turnover: a long term view.
4. Worldwide proprietary research and,
5. (Most importantly) patience and confidence in the capitalist system.

We hope the enclosed history of Bear markets will alert you that the best time to invest is when you decide that a Professional, operating amidst a consistent, dynamic culture, can perform in the investment arena better than a do-it-yourself amateur. Sorry, but when a person decides to make his own investment decisions, he or she becomes his/her own investment advisor.

Sincerely yours,
The Omega Financial Group

Subject: Early warning & letters are coming

We don't know about our readers, but quite honestly, we are fed up with hearing the Obama Administration in Washington say the answer to the financial problems in our country is to "tax the rich." We intend in the very near future to produce a white paper which will go into further detail about this very same mantra coming from the Administration and the Left. We hope to answer some questions and even to raise some questions about this consistent drum beat streaming from Pennsylvania Avenue.

"Sooner or later—Here comes the Drum Major." —BAO

President Obama, in a budget speech a few weeks ago, indicated that if the wealthiest Americans were asked to "pay a little more", and they did it, our fiscal problems would vanish. If that happened it would be one of the most sterling, mind bending miracles that any politician could pull off. Somewhere somebody said, "say it enough and sooner or later people will believe it."

As all of us know, the Republicans are insisting the problem is not lack of revenues it's too much spending. They rightly point out that if we increase revenues with more taxes and do not reduce spending we're right back where we started: having to raise the debt limit year after year, decade after decade, until finally the whole thing explodes and nobody will loan us money. If they do, it will be at a skyrocketing interest rate.

In a recent *Review and Outlook* column in *The Wall Street Journal,* the editorial writers presented its readers with a thought experiment. While we are certain that the editorial writers do not want to encourage the Democrats to take up any *new* ideas, here's a summary of the *Journal* hypothetical.

"Read these two paragraphs carefully!"

The last income tax statistics available from the Internal Revenue Service is for 2008. From this data we discovered that the top 1% of tax payers—those with salaries, dividends, and capital gains, roughly above $380,000 paid 38% of income taxes. While 2008 was not a boom year, here's what the *Journal's* editorial hypothecated: Assume the tax policy **confiscated** 100% and put *all of the income of all the "millionaires and billionaires"* that Mr. Obama singled out in this recent speech, into the hands of the IRS; those calculations showed that it would yield about $938 billion which is not a drop in the bucket to the 4 trillion dollar White House budget. This unthinkable budget is a $1.65 trillion deficit and represents spending at 25% as a share of the *economy,* which by the way is a post WWII record.

In the *Journal's* hypo, they further visualize taking 100% of the income from the top 10% of taxpayers where everyone with income over $114,000 (including joint filers), supplies the juice The data was broken down by the Journal at a rounded out $100,000; if you taxed all income 100% above that level it would throw off only $3.4 trillion. Interestingly enough, the top 10% already pay 60% of all total income taxes. By the way, the top 5% pay more than all of the other 95%. This does not include Social Security and Medicare dollars flowing into the Administration's "lock box", most of which finally to be traded for Treasury Bonds issued by the U.S. Government. (So much for the "lock box" theory!)

Truth That Will Last

However, these facts do not silence the story we hear over and over again that the answer to the fiscal problems in this country is to simply insist on the wealthy, and higher income people to pay more taxes. Since we know the numbers shown don't consider Medicare, Medicaid, and Social Security, it is obvious that the cost of those entitlements is expected to grow rapidly in the future. With more and more baby boomers "joining the crowd" daily, it's impossible for the "rich" to finance Mr. Obama's entitlement ambitions even *before* his Health Care plan kicks in. So where does the Administration claim the money will come from? This same voice we hear regarding the taxing of the "wealthy" refuses to mention the "third rail": the **Middle Class**.

The only place the IRS can go to get more money than they're getting now with tax increases is from the people making from $50,000 to $200,000 per year: the Middle Class. Going back to 2008 the IRS records show that there's about $5.65 trillion in total *taxable income from all individual tax payers*, and most of that came from middle income earners.

"Don't kid yourself—it will eventually crumble!"

As Mr. Obama is aware, it's political suicide for the President to tell the voting public that in order to come close to getting enough revenue to make a "fake effort" to balance the budget would be to tax the middle income tax payers. What has always happened in the past is exactly what we believe the Obama Administration has in mind. Limiting "tax deductions and other loop holes", such as mortgage interest payments, would provide extra money, which according to the Administration will reduce the deficit. However, we all know from past history this tactic would simply enable uncontrolled spending by our Federal Government. When you add in the other "loop holes" such as excluding deductions for state and local tax payments, which includes property taxes, mortgage interest, employers sponsored health insurance, 401(k) contributions, and certain charitable donations, it still would not give us leverage to decrease the velocity of the spending machine in Washington. And make no mistake: this mad spending spree can't *all* be laid at the feet of the Democrats.

So if we want to help erase the fiscal mess that our country is in, before election day 2012, there has to be a bi partisan drive to cut out some spending even if it pains us on the home front.

Our belief is that the American people are ready to make sacrifices, providing the Federal, state and even city governments are willing to do the same thing. Let's hope that it doesn't take a constitutional amendment for a balanced budget to solve our problem and that our elected officials will belly up and do what needs to be done to solve this ever growing problem.

There are sensible ways to escape this coming train wreck. And there are sensible people in both political parties.

A New Old Idea—2-D Investing
During the recent worldwide stock market decline, conventional thinking says that by being diversified in various sectors or areas (international and global stocks; bonds; domestic stocks large and small) would cushion the downturn, this time it didn't. All markets were hit. The only investment that was safe and stable was US Government Securities.

During times such as this, many advisors moved their clients to bonds (government or corporate) or cash. This solved the existing problem by "stopping the bleeding"; however, it would be quite difficult to move back into the market at the most opportune time. And one also had to get out of the market at the perfect time, which is just as difficult to accomplish.

In the early 1970s Carl Andersen, a Boston colleague, and I, came up with a program which made a big difference in our client's portfolios. We called it "Two-Dimensional" investing.

"So how does it work?"

Depositing sums of money into bond funds which were at that time paying interest (dividends) in double digits, we directed the monthly cash dividends over into either growth or growth and income funds which had declined in value with the Bear Market of 1974. This cash flow allowed our clients to "dollar cost average" with this income the bonds produced. When the market turned, the plan was to move the money from the bonds to the stock funds. Easier said than done!

"Oops!"

Since a bell did not ring and signal the bottom of the market, we were "whipsawed" a few times by even another sudden downturn!

As the years passed we found Equity Income and Balanced funds which held not only a fair supply of higher yielding bonds, but had large concentrations of dividend paying stocks, which not only pro-vided a package with a modicum of safety but also made it possible for the investor to stay invested in both the Equity Income funds (the producing side) and the receiving side (growth and income funds) and not miss the market's upswing. Although there are other advantages to "Two-Dimensional" investing we recognize that by using this approach we do not get pure safety. But the upside is the knowledge that your portfolio is in a position to recover lost ground without attempting to guess right about stock markets moves. As we've said: "No one knows where the bottom lies."

Sincerely,
The Omega Financial Group

2011 Concept

Fifth White Paper
Risk Management Utilizing Alternative Investments

It's been almost 3 years since we've expressed to our clients, and other interested parties, what we believe might transpire over the intermediate term in regard to the global economy and our investment concepts.

It was in 2009 that we brought to your attention a phrase coined by Mr. Bill Gross and Mr. Mohamed El-Erian of the PIMCO organization, tagged "The New Normal." Quite a number of commentators throughout our industry and market observers didn't take much notice to this concept. But, after research and reasoned observations, we came to believe this economic path made sense. Debt exhaustion and poorly capitalized activities were immediately pointed out, but the main reason was the deleveraging of individuals and businesses both in the United States and abroad which has caused considerable collateral damage to the global economy. As we said in 2009, it all started with the demise of Lehman Brothers in mid September 2008.

Another situation that has arisen that is lesser known to the general public, is the confusing results of the Dodd-Frank financial edict put forth by congress in an attempt to quell the panic and negate the economic explosions during the end of the last decade. Following this major downturn we observed that markets, households, institutional and government policies have played a major role in increasing the speed of these more volatile markets; The lower market returns during the last 3 years have prompted us to stand by our convictions that global markets will not give us in the immediate future the dramatic growth that we experienced in the 1980s and 1990s.

Quoting Mr. El-Erian, co-CIO of PIMCO, "The world has changed in a manner that is unlikely to be reversed over the next few years. Put another way, markets are recovering from a shock that goes way, way beyond a cyclical flesh wound." Interesting how this prediction made by Mr. El-Erian at PIMCO in 2006 has come about. We have seen since the downturn of 2008 and 2009 (and the sharp recovery in the spring of 2009) government intervention in re-regulating and putting pressure on the international banking system. The securities industry that services some 50% of the U.S. population with investment concepts is closely tied to the banking business. As we have pointed out, the Glass-Steagall Act, which demolished the wall between commercial banking and stock brokerage, has created scores of disappointments in investment results of individuals and companies.

We'll not attempt in this essay to cover all the pitfalls and strong volatility of the last several years. We hope rather to address once again some opportunities we've found during this past conflict, which could help us guide a number of our clients through the swampland of uncertainty.

As many of you remember from our other white papers, we have determined that the avenue of mutual fund investing is the road we have chosen to present to clients who fit our profile of global investing. The concept of utilizing alternative investments has triggered the necessity of seeking out and utilizing types of funds which attempt to react in opposite directions from stock and equity markets in our clients' portfolios.

In order to be useful, alternative investments really must accomplish at least three things; they need to represent a source of return independent of traditional asset classes (stocks, bonds). They should possess volatility characteristics that are tolerable for the end investor (the client), and they should offer negative correlation characteristics of stock and bond investments. Most of the alternatives we've chosen, even through the most recent downturns, have demonstrated their ability to do just that. By wisely spreading assets among diversified classes—large cap growth, small cap growth/value, various global allocations, and the proper bond mix, we've managed to cushion some of the downturn in portfolios where previously lay nothing but common stock funds, and conventional bond funds.

We all know that if you suffer a 50% decline in a portfolio, you have to subsequently have that portfolio increase by 100% in order to get back to your starting point. **So in terms of long term investment success, getting a handle on portfolio volatility and attempting to manage risk and avoiding negative similar returns, alternatives are really indispensable.**

As you know, we strongly believe that while giving up a small percentage of upside growth possibility, we should always keep a meaningful equity position in the portfolio. Additionally, we prefer dividend paying funds which help to not only cushion downturns, but increase the asset accumulation.

In order to meet the volatile moves of those markets, we discovered it was necessary to provide some sort of commodity and foreign currency representation in the portfolio. We've understood for a long time that the use of TIPS (Treasury Inflation Protection Securities) helps to hedge certain market downturns, caused by price inflation.

Another example of vehicles that weren't available 10 to 15 years ago, are funds that have been designed to "short" the market which have proven to act as a flexible hedge during times of extreme bear market volatility.

Next is the question of hedging risk. Anytime you can utilize a small but reasonable percentage of a portfolio featuring alternative investments, especially in the form of mutual funds, you've strengthened the hedge. So rather than utilize some trick of market timing and liquidating stock funds 100% during a bear market and going to cash, we prefer to keep smaller amounts in various alternative investments in order to be fully invested in stock funds when the market turns (and they seem to turn more rapidly these days than they have in the past!). We have attempted in our search for the proper strategy to use money market funds, and mutual funds which feature short sales, and other non correlated equity assets to mitigate downside risk. Our goal is to attempt to manage risk at the advisory level. Unlike adding to the risk of our client's portfolios by attempting to time these markets, we prefer at the onset to express to our clients that our first task is to enlighten them that if they want to participate in the market's upside, we must protect those portfolios on the downside. **We've never met anyone who knows when to exit the market and when to return to it.**

In the long run, historically, equity, both domestic and global, always end up being our core investment vehicle. We believe that a positive and well managed stock portfolio has always won in the long run. Rather than go into the explanation of why (we'll cover our thoughts on that in another paper) we'll simply say that our goal is to be sure that our clients are allocated in strong equity funds.

We have long admired and utilized those managed by Capital Research and Management (American Funds), Franklin Templeton Funds, and other newer consistent, conservative, long term visualizing fund groups such as the PIMCO group. However, we think that alternative funds should represent 10% to 30% of the portfolio, depending on the markets.

The secret of course, is no secret! As we pointed out in the 2009 paper on alternatives, "These investments must have a low correlation with equity and bond markets." **In other words, when stock markets go down an alternative investment is designed to go up, and vice versa.** So rather than utilize pure high risk and expensive hedge funds, we initiate more conservative funds which "hedge" on a minor basis against those down markets; still providing conservative, dividend paying equity funds, both domestic and international, so that a portfolio will be in place when the market turns.

Creative Allocations

A few innovative fund companies have brought to the market place a two pronged fund which by using a small percentage of the portfolio in equity indexed funds, with a major "backup" in short term bonds, can be utilized to reduce volatility and still be open for a bull market. This has lowered the volatility factor during the shaky times during the first decade of the 21st Century. Perhaps the major advantage of this approach is being able to funnel the dividends on a dollar cost averaging basis during volatile periods.

Many of you are aware that we, at Omega Securities Inc., have formed an additional organization called Omega Wealth Partners Inc., which is open to accounts that have a minimum value of $500,000. However, we are still able to utilize these alternative investments in accounts which hold fewer assets. We hope if you have some interest in learning more about how we do this, that you will take the time to scan our website, www.omegawp.com. There are various links that you can utilize to give you our ideas of managing risk. Risk is no longer a bad word, but has become a necessity to manage if we are to outstrip inflation. Downside protection will help you to accomplish your long term goals and hopefully sleep easier at night.

SECTION III

Opinions

We have included, in the final section, a miscellaneous group of editorial comments that we've labeled **OPINIONS**. These articles represent various events which have occurred prior to or during the time of publication. Some Opinion pieces cover controversial events occurring under the umbrella of governments local, national and/or international. These Opinion columns sometimes attempt to point out, both government and business events which might take advantage of the participating public. We have dated these editorials to give you a time picture of the event. All of the Opinions are our own.

Spring/Summer 2002
Our Opinion

What's My Line?

Recently, we read an article by Anita Faulkner from a newsletter put out by the Sycamore Financial Group in Kokomo, Indiana. Craig Smith is the Broker/Dealer and an old acquaintance of mine. We thought we'd share it.

During the 1960s, the popular TV show, "What's My Line?" had celebrities guess the professions of ordinary people. With the following clues, can you guess what the people below have in common?

1. These people live well below their financial means.
2. These people allocate time, energy and money in ways that build wealth.
3. These people believe that financial independence is more important than displaying high social status.
4. Their parents did not provide economic outpatient care.
5. Their adult children are economically self-sufficient.
6. These people are proficient in targeting market opportunities.
7. These people chose the right occupations.

The seven attributes listed above apply to "self-made" millionaires. In a recent survey of 1,115 millionaires in the U.S., these are the common denominators of financial independence achieved by hard work, perseverance, planning, and self-discipline. More often than not, the men and women who accumulate great wealth have one thing in common, a simple lifestyle.

The millionaires in the survey were, by and large, small business owners who had typically lived in the same town for all of their adult lives. They live next door to people with a fraction of their wealth. They don't wear expensive clothes or drive new cars; their homes are relatively modest compared to their financial status.

In a nutshell, simple living is about choice. People who live simply are in control of their money and their lives. When we buy into Madison Avenue advertising campaigns, we spend our choices. Financial independence is a lifestyle that buys control of how and where you will spend your time.

Late Winter 2002
Our Opinion

"Same Song, Second Verse"

Recently, *The Wall Street Journal* posted an interesting chart—a study entitled "Moving Up?" The Journal points out that actual research tracking the wages of more than 180,000 Californians from 1988 to 2000 showed that people in all groups move up the economic ladder and the "real wage gains were greatest for those workers who started out at the lowest wages." Below you will see how this stacks up.

Moving On Up—Median annual earnings of actual California workers

Workers who started in this quintile	Started with these earnings in 1988	Were earning this by 2000
Bottom Quintile	$13,136	$27,194
2nd Quintile	$25,476	$32,837
Middle Quintile	$36,874	$42,410
4th Quintile	$51,177	$56,013
Top Quintile	$74,826	$80,209
Source: Sphere Institute		

The gloom-and-doomers who always see a full scale class war when it comes to economic status and those who would like to instigate that class war should take a look at the actual statistics shown by this California survey. In the bottom quintile you'll notice that in 1988, the average income was $13,136. By the year 2000 that bottom quintile was earning $27,194. These were not estimates. The survey utilized data from individual people. Anyway, I think you see the point.

As long as we live in a free society and have the ability to move from one occupation to the other and have the opportunity to get an education, we can improve the chances to increase our income. Thus we are playing out the American dream which says that the "Poor get Richer."

That's our take. Yours is welcome.

Early Winter 2002
Our Opinion

Tax the rich! They never pay enough taxes."
Were you aware that the top one percent of all earners in 1999 earned 19.5% of all adjusted gross income reported to the IRS, yet they paid 32.2% of all federal income taxes that year? YEP! The "super rich" pay in taxes nearly double their proportion of national income. Take a look at the table shown below and see who is financing this government. About twenty years ago the "super-rich" paid only 19% of all federal income taxes. By 1991, thanks to the progressive impact of the Reagan tax-cuts, that share had climbed to 24.8% and by 1999 it was above 36%. The story is the same for the merely "filthy-rich", the top 5% of filers, who according to *The Wall Street Journal*, paid 43.4% of all taxes in 1991, but by 1999 paid 55.5%.

We wonder how the government will make it since the top income tax rate has been cut from 39.6% to 35%. However, maybe we can squeeze by for a while because that doesn't go into effect until 2006.

Current Comment
Winter 2013

...And regarding the above tax brackets—Don't worry. The tax has gone up to 39.6% for earners over $400,000. And according to the Obama Administration, *"It's only just begun."*

Who's Paying Taxes in 1999		
Percentiles	Total Share of AGI	Total Share of AGI% of Federal Personal Income Tax
Top 1%	19.50%	36.20%
Top 5%	34.00%	55.50%
Top 10%	44.90%	66.50%
Top 25%	66.50%	83.50%
Top 50%	8680.00%	96.00%
Bottom 50%	13.20%	4.00%
Source IRS *Ranked by adjusted gross income (AGI)		

"Who are the wealthy?"

According to *The Wall Street Journal* and the 1999 IRS numbers, all you had to earn to be among the top 25% of all tax filers was a whooping $52,965. To be among the top 50% you had to earn only $26,415. The interesting thing about this number is that many of these average people are tomorrow's wealthy. According to an analysis of the University of Michigan for the period from 1975-1991, more than 80% of the families who started in the lowest 1/5 of earning population, had moved to middle-class incomes, earning an average that last year of 1991 of $22,304 or above.

"Most are new consumers"

You see the great thing about a capitalistic society is that income mobility means that people are not stuck in the same tax-bracket.

Washington wants voters to believe that the only people being taxed at these high rates are the Trumps and the Rockefellers. What really happens is that the higher rates end up soaking essentially middle-class people, whose incomes rise during their careers until they end up paying the same tax rates as the Kennedy's, though they still can't afford to sail off Cape Cod.

That's our take, yours is welcome.

Winter 1992
Our Opinion

War and Peace/Bull and Bear Markets

In the 1990/1991 Persian Gulf War, most people were selling their stocks. Wise investors were buying, likewise in the 1987 crash and the 1994 downturn.

It takes wisdom and courage to recognize that bull markets will not last forever. But it takes even more strength to look past down-markets and see the next upturn.

Mark Helprin in a recent *Wall Street Journal* op-ed piece describes the office of the President of the United States in similar terms:

> *"It is difficult for individuals or nations to recognize that war and peace alternate. But they do. No matter how long peace may last, it will end in war …The Statesman… will, in the midst of common despair, see the end of war, just as during the peace he was alive to the inevitability of war…"*

So remember: markets will inevitably fall. A decline in stock prices is a sure thing. The key thing here is for smart, experienced, and courageous money managers to step up and find the bargains. And, hopefully, that's what our managers are doing right now.

That's our take. Yours is welcome.

Mr. Steagall—The "Glass" is Broken

November 1999 witnessed a historical event. Congress sent President Clinton a bill that reshaped the financial landscape of our country. Utilizing "buggy whip" journalistic mentality, the media calls the wall between banks, insurance companies and investment firms a "Depression-era barrier." Under the guise that it is for the "good of the public," Congress has done away with the Glass-Steagall Act.

Intoxicated by soft money and campaign contributions, the Senate overwhelmingly voted 90–8 in support of the bill. This landmark legislation effectively allows banks, brokerage firms and insurance companies to merge into one "financial service" conglomerate. Naturally, the banking community is the driving force here. They have convinced the media and our elected legislators that the government oversight of the past is not needed.

President Clinton said in a statement that the bill "will help the American financial services system play a leading role in propelling our economy into the 21st Century.…" Other voices, however, sing a different song: Senator Paul Wellstone, D-Minnesota, during a Senate debate, rightfully observed that the measure would bring "the concentration of more and more economic power into the hands of fewer and fewer people." Other representatives called the bill a "consumer fraud masquerading as financial reform."

Just think of it, you can go to one place, deposit your paycheck; pay your bills; buy your stocks or mutual funds; purchase life insurance and buy a policy covering your teenage son's car.

"You like this? Just wait for Obamacare!"

You can probably tell by the tone of this article that we totally oppose this new legislation. With apologies to our friends in the banking business, we are reminded of the old statement which I'm sorry to say now applies to the Big Banks: "I'm from the IRS and I'm here to help you."

Mid Spring 2008 – (and then we wrote...)
Our Opinion

The crumbling of the wall between Banking and Securities has faded into an amalgamate which blended the two into an almost unrecognized entity. With the Federal Reserve pledged to maintain the safety of markets through oversight of bank holding companies, they now have opened up financing to a number of securities firms, through its discount windows. This is the warning bell that the wall has not only crumbled, it has turned to dust. When is a "bailout" not a "bailout?"

Remember the days when a banker made a loan and kept it on his books and didn't have the accounting freedom to throw it away as an "off balance sheet item?"

While we would hardly find ourselves cheering the Super Regulators, we wonder what entity will end up regulating and supervising the "new" complex business models that trade in unregistered securities, and other shadowy investment vehicles: the Federal Reserve, the SEC or a new and costly bureaucracy.

Make no mistake. The greed of the big investment banks on Wall Street will come back to haunt them and this will affect free markets worldwide.

In spite of this, a free trading economy and capital markets can find new ways to continue to finance the growth industries, not only in the US, but worldwide. As the subprime mortgage package unwinds and hopefully, less greedy bankers emerge, we believe that our investors will hold on, add more to their portfolio and relinquish to our professionals the freedom to operate consistently as they have since 1934.

That's our take. Yours is welcome.

One of the ads that we run in the *Fort Worth Star-Telegram* on a bi-monthly basis makes a clear and obvious statement: "A down market is the price you pay for exceptional returns." This is not just something that we quote; it's something that we believe.

There is no way that your wealth can grow, unless there is a chance that the price of your stocks will go down so that bargains can be obtained when people with less patience sell in a panic during a down market. Believe us, there is no way that the markets for stocks anywhere in the world will consistently continue to return 20% a year. We've quoted that in these pages so many times, that by now, there shouldn't be any questions about what we believe. Thankfully, we get very few phone calls from our clients being concerned about markets asking, "Should we sell at this time?"

What is difficult to remember is that everyone who accepts market volatility and who understands that markets for stocks can go up also has recognized one time or another in their life that they also can go down. Many times we forget that recognition and forget the fact that we know that they can go down. But no matter what anybody says or thinks, they really know that markets for stocks can go both ways.

"So what about the pros?"

We have found that the secret, especially when it comes to professional management, is to employ people, who not only have brains, organization, and research facilities, but also the courage to do the thing that's right with you and your money. Thus far this year, we've faced some big down days and some of our clients have expressed some concerns. When you consider that all the economic ingredients for a positive future are there, you need to be assured that the real professionals who are managing your money have the courage to pull the trigger when things just don't "feel" right. And in this business, you either pull the trigger at the right time, or you miss the target completely. The deal, of course, is to let the professional make the decision.

Keep the faith; understand that our free market system always will have volatility. There will always be those who are less courageous than you, who will always sell at the bottom and scramble to buy at the top.

That's our take. Yours is welcome.

Spring 2003
Our Opinion

As evidenced by many former employees of Enron and WorldCom, you can definitely get rich by not diversifying, but we've also found out that you can't stay rich by not diversifying. Almost every client we have asks us, "What do you think the market will do?"—or, better still, "What is the market doing now?" These, of course, are questions that we can't answer because not only do we not know, but we're really not as interested in markets as we are in companies. We also become highly cognizant of people who manage the money that our clients entrust to us.

Many investment advisors, without core beliefs, simply sell the client what makes the client feel good. For example, many online brokers have changed their advertising schemes three or four times in the last 6 months. This is caused from a basic lack of core belief. It is very difficult on us as advisors not to yield to the temptation of instant gratification as opposed to investing for the future.

There are Really Only Two Ways to Look at Investing When it Comes to Anticipating the Future…

The first way is to be convinced that the future financing of American Industry and the free enterprise system will be based on bonds (borrowing) rather than equities (owning). If you believe that people will no longer be willing to take some sort of risk for future returns, then you should probably become a bond

investor. However, if you believe as we do, that American markets will grow because entrepreneurs are willing to take risks—then you should have a portion of your portfolio in common stocks.

That's our take. Yours is welcome.

June 1998
Our Opinion

For years we have advocated both to our clients and in these columns that the most important thing when it comes to buying mutual funds is that it's not the cost of buying, it's the cost of owning that's important.

Of all the domestic stock funds charted by Morningstar, Inc., the average expense ratio is 1.40% per year (i.e., $140 per year for every $10,000 invested). The international funds they track cost 1.85%.

Far and away our largest amount of money under management is domestic stock funds. Our average annual expense ratio in that group is 0.71% ($71 for each $10,000 under management) and on the International side our cost is 0.95% vs. 1.85%.

As you can see, all things being equal, it doesn't take long for that discrepancy to make a difference in results. And over longer periods of time, 10 or 15 years, it makes a great deal of difference. So remember:

It's not what it costs to buy, it's what it costs to own that is most important.

That's our take. Yours is welcome.

September 1998
Our Opinion

On August 31, 1998, after flipping on my television set I was reminded that CNBC, the stock market TV channel, reminded me a lot of ESPN, the all-sports station. (This was the Monday that the market for stocks dropped 500+ points.)

Here was the deep-voiced announcer as the anchor covering the "Big Game." Alongside this well-dressed guy were a couple of analysts explaining the "plays." The "score" (Dow Jones Industrial Average and the S&P 500 Stock Index) blinks at us in a little box on the corner of the screen. Then there's the proverbial "sideline" analyst stationed on the New York Stock Exchange floor, speaking in a loud, high-pitched voice to overcome the surrounding confusion and noise. (I kept waiting for an interview with Troy Aikman.) And, of course, after the required commercials, here came the guest commentators: economists, brokerage firm VPs, and fund managers all giving us their take on the "Big Game."

ALL VERY EXCITING, BUT THERE IS ONE PROBLEM: INVESTING IS NOT A "GAME."

In our opinion, investing is research and hard work and maybe not a lot of fun. Investing means using intelligence and sound judgment. It means understanding that, as a manager of money, there is a sense of moral if not fiduciary responsibility to the shareholder.

In short, we here at Omega take our work seriously and endeavor to see what your dreams and goals are. We do not take investing as a game. And neither should you.

So the next time you tune into the "Big Game," do yourself a favor: change channels.

Remember: the best investment for you may not be the best for your neighbor. And the best one for you is one you can hold onto in all types of markets.

That's our take. Yours is welcome.

"What's Good for General Motors is Good for the USA… Maybe"

I was asked recently by a friend, who believes that big is good, if I thought small investment firms (such as Omega Securities) and their clients would be swallowed up by the big ones. I have mulled that over in my mind and had begun to try to answer that question to myself for obvious reasons.

I was quite concerned until a recent visit to New York City allowed me to walk up and down Madison and Park Avenue and some of the side streets. Here I would see small jewelry stores, clothing boutiques, and shops that sell only men's ties. Here were stores selling clothes offering only one brand and eyeglass shops which would sell one brand of glasses. Why haven't these unique shops been swallowed up by the Nordstrom's, the Dillard's, and the Macy's?

Here's what I think. I believe people want to deal with people who have a "stake" in their business. There will always be a place for the specialty shops where the individual comes before the company. Confidence and trust are most important, especially when dealing with finances.

Yes, Virginia. We believe the small boutiques will not only survive but will prosper. And that includes Omega Securities."

That's my take. Yours is welcome.

December 1998
My Opinion

Congress's expansion of retirement plans is probably the only major change we'll see in the near future. Addressing social security is virtually impossible for the politicians to do unless they are pushed to the wall politically. Usually when this happens all that Congress knows is raise taxes (definition of "saving Social Security").

Both Republicans and Democrats have relied on increasing tax revenues to fund their pet projects for so long that the idea of cutting taxes or allowing individual Americans to invest part of their social security taxes in equities just doesn't seem to fit their mind set. And with more and more commerce being conducted on the internet where prying IRS agents can't see, the crunch will come soon. This will lead to downsizing the government; hopefully sooner rather than later.

Freedom is a wondrous thing. If only our leadership could recognize it.

That's our take. Yours is welcome.

March 1999
Our Opinion

The Information Age is here for sure. For most people there is a definite place for your money in technology funds. However, the stocks in the portfolio should be reasonably priced. That's what the people managing your money believe. This Information Age will, we believe, be a period of important growth in our living standard, and institutional improvements will leave people freer than they are today. We believe that big government will shrink and be less susceptible to failures than large scale centralized command systems; all due to improved communication which breeds the new worldwide resource: knowledge. We know that water, land, and other such resources are finite, while knowledge in the Information Age can be leveraged and in turn holds out to be practically infinite.

That's our opinion. Yours is welcome.

Our Opinion

With all of the obviously positive news that we have given you in this addition of *Opinions & Facts*, you may wonder why we constantly alert you on these pages that you should not look for overnight riches. Why do we warn you that you should keep your focus long-term, no matter what your age? We do this to help you stay the course.

"Thanks. My mother told me that when I was a kid."

The main reason investment plans do not work is the undoing of the plan by either the planner or the investor. You see, the most natural thing in the world is to buy securities and not hold on when markets go down. It's almost an American credo.

Inexperience in volatile markets is as bad a malady among investment planners as among investors.

It is our role to be certain your investment plan fits your personality and allows you to sleep well. It is our role to put your investments with the finest managers world-wide; managers who have weathered all sorts of storms in financial markets. But most important, it is our responsibility to really care about your future and the future of your children and grandchildren.

You may find other programs that appear to take care of all of your needs at a lower cost, but rest assured that the well-being of your financial future is in the excellent, experienced hands of people who truly care.

That's our opinion. Yours is welcome.

June 1999
Our Opinion

There's no question about it. We're living in an era of a "new economy." But, if you've taken half a glance, you've discovered that this new economy has not brought permanent happiness and bliss. Nor will your investment account continue to grow at high double-digit rates for the next decade.

Housing and autos use to drive the economy; now information technology accounts for one-quarter to one-third of economic growth. In Silicon Valley, eleven new companies are created every week, and, on average, a Silicon Valley company goes public every five days, meaning dozens of new millionaires.

Another aspect of the new economy is globalization. Imports and exports make up more than 25% of our economic activity. We all must face the fact that wages will soon be linked to cost structures and other nations' competing job markets. This raises living standards all over the world as a way of keeping inflation in check.

While we'd love to see wages go up in the U.S., the only way this will happen is through improved productivity, not wage negotiations. Improved productivity means a worker must continue to educate herself and step into the swift waters of the Information Age. Uncomfortable for some of us? No question.

So here we are ankle deep in fast moving commerce and wondering how it all will end. The answer seems to be that we must provide more and better education for our workforce and face the fact that we have more competition both here and overseas.

This, of course, is what makes free market capitalism work.

That's our opinion. Yours is welcome.

October 1999
Our Opinion

At long last the Texas weather has broken. Feels like Southern California without the ocean. By the same token, the retreat of the stock market, anticipated by some of us since 1995, has finally happened. No one knows or ever will know enough to accurately predict the duration of the bear or bull markets. But we have learned over the years and have repeated it on these pages time and again.

A tree does not grow to the sky.

Down markets will occur.

Local and national media covered one of the most unbelievable statements I've heard of in recent years on Friday, September 24, 1999. Microsoft President Stephen Balmer, addressing a conference in Seattle of the Society of American Business Editors and Writers, cited what he called a "god rush" mentality that had driven the market far too high.

Said Balmer, "It's bad whenever reality is out of line, and you get distortions which are not healthy." He went on to say that there is tremendous overvaluation of technology stocks. Then he said, "And, I'd put my company's stock in that category."

Well, duh! With Microsoft trading at a PE ratio in the 60s and eyeballing other dotcoms trading in the stratosphere, we've been wondering how long it was going to take sensible people to wake up to the fact that this stock market has been overpriced for quite some time.

Usually what happens in these cases (35 years of experience has given us firsthand knowledge), is that the people who've been throwing money at overpriced stocks will now go overboard, panic sell to the point where the stocks are not just reasonably priced but below their actual value. At least that's what sensible investors hope happens.

The majority of the money managers that we recommend are sitting on nice stacks of cash waiting for the amateurs to throw their portfolios to the wolves. This is how it works, haw it has always worked and how it will always work.

That's our opinion. Yours is welcome.

August 1999
Our Opinion

It's interesting to note that purchases of shares in stock mutual funds are down almost 50% from a year ago, and many funds are experiencing net withdrawals. More than likely, the money is going into individual stocks as people bypass traditional mutual funds in favor of online trading and internet research. What's really happening in this case is that people are no longer happy with the double-digit returns mutual funds have made and have become enamored with the frenzy and drive for internet stocks. A very high percentage of mutual fund shareholders have never experienced a down market. We find it truly amazing that these people who have never gone through this undeniably painful experience would believe they have more expertise in managing money than those who have devoted the major part of their life to it.

The culture of the '90s has convinced many Americans that it is essential that "you do it on your own." This is, of course, the Great Lie of the decade. The internet, a fountain of information, does not carry with it the dose of wisdom needed to reach investment goals. Intimidated by the Great Lie, these "do it yourselfers" will eventually stumble. Let's pray it happens before it is too late to recover."

That's our take. Yours is welcome

June 2000

Opinion - March 2000
"Carl, We Hardly Knew Ye"

My friend Carl Andersen refers to the day-traders and anyone who thinks that investing is easy as "unwashed investors," AKA "Internet Bears" those who've never lived through a Bear market which lasted longer than a night's sleep.

Carl points out in a recent communiqué that the auto industry started with around 250 innovators, schemers, and dreamers and now numbers three: General Motors, Ford, and, of course Chrysler, which is now German! So the survival rate among 250 of these auto companies is two or 0.8%.

Only about eleven of the top Internet group have growing operating revenues. In some cases actual earnings have gone down an average of 53.3% over the fifty-two weeks ending April 20. The ones who may stay have marketing clout and money to expand their operations. When these high risk, highly valuated, Internet driven operations crater, only a few will survive.

And finally... our opinion.

That's an easy one. You need expert investment advice. You need confidence and trust in the people who've been around for a long time and have been through down markets.

Our economy is roaring on and we are only at the start of the information revolution. So you can bet that over the long hall, the well managed, well run companies in this country and overseas will prosper. But as people buy stocks on the Internet having absolutely no idea as to what the company does or whether it makes any money, you can look for a bad hangover.

And a parting thought...

When the lottery dollars get big, big, everybody rushes to buy. But have you noticed that the week after the drawing and somebody wins, hardly anybody buys. The same goes after the bubble bursts...nobody buys.

That's our take. Yours is welcome.

April 2001
Our Opinion

Senator Pete Domenici (R) N.M. has now indicated that maybe only a 4% increase in the Federal budget would somehow be able to work. Only a couple of weeks ago he was worried the government would crash under these austere budgetary restraints. And talk about changes, have you ever seen anybody change the way the Democrats have regarding tax cuts. I won't get into all the details but just as it happened in the Clinton years; it looks like the Democrats have suddenly changed their name tags to read Republican. So in the middle of this, our friend Senator Joe Lieberman (D) Conn. has said that the government should write a $300 check and send it to everybody in the United States. I'm assuming he means the people who pay taxes, but then again maybe he means everybody in the United States.

"No kidding! President Carter actually did recommend the $50 rebate!"

This reminds me of the Jimmy Carter $50 tax rebate. This was his method to cure stagflation by refunding taxpayers $50 each who didn't pay taxes. Of course that notion was laughed out of Congress when people started comparing it to stimulating the economy by scattering $50 bills from airplanes.

In a recent op-ed *Wall Street Journal* piece, Robert L Bartley points out that the Carter $50 rebate came along when people still believed in the Keynesian "multiplier effect." By putting money in people pockets, the reasoning was that the government would "inject" money whether from higher spending or lower taxes and it would be "multiplied" many times at the higher gross domestic product. Since then, of course, Keynesian economics stumbled mainly on the sticky question of where the government gets the money it "injects."

"Where does the money come from? Are you kidding me? There's not but two places...either you borrow it or you steal it."

This brings us to our point: The government does not put money in our pockets; it takes it out of some pockets and puts it in others. If the government writes checks for $60 billion in tax rebates, as Senator Lieberman is suggesting, it will borrow $60 billion more, or pay back $60 billion less in debt. Pray tell us how these offsetting transactions are supposed to stimulate anything.

The only long-term answer is to build an incentive for people to work harder and earn more money without paying more taxes. These incentives are basically measured by marginal tax rates. That's the tax we pay on an additional dollar of earnings. President Bush's plan is to cut the highest marginal rates. In a progressive income tax structure the highest marginal rates generally apply to taxpayers with high income. If you want economic stimulus you've got to cut the top marginal rates to increase incentives for your most productive

citizens. This of course, does not play well politically, but if Bush hangs tough, you'll see the next level of this economic boom explode us into the next decade, providing we control spending in Washington. We have hammered in these lines and these newsletters, in the 1980's when the marginal tax rates were cut, it set off a great financial and economic boom that is still going on today.

That's our take. Yours is welcome.

Current Comment—2013
Dream on: Mr. Obama won the election. Thanks for the memories.

From A September 2001 *Wall Street Journal Opinion & Facts* **Piece**
9/11/01
Our Opinion

One of the most positive things to come out of the tragedy in New York and Washington is that both sides of the aisle, the Republicans and the Democrats, seem to be on a unified course as are, as we've observed, many Americans.

It is with this determination and drive that our country has evolved as the leader of the world in democracy, peace, diplomacy and economic growth. The courage of all those responding to the tragedy is to be cheered and applauded.

The terrorists have unleashed a sleeping powerful machine and it will turn out to be one of the biggest mistakes made in the history of mankind. We all have discovered that you cannot legislate patriotism. Patriotism comes from events that open a wellspring deep within each American which, although we may not realize it, has been there all along. It was born when our forefathers broke from their English chains, established a Constitution of Freedom and began to exercise that freedom in a God given land. Nurtured with the blood of the Civil War and in France's trenches during World War I, it hardened in the battles on two sides of the globe during the second World War, and then resurfaced on the frozen tundra of North Korea. It grew stronger in the sweltering jungles of Southeast Asia. This patriotic endeavor manifests itself in the ruins of the World Trade Center with the first heroes of the 3rd World War. The nobility of the American spirit will never be quenched, because out of all of this comes the recognition that all men are created equal no matter their color or creed or how they spell their last name.

And now we face another more formidable task: an enemy that we cannot see. An enemy who has no geographical boundaries, one which strikes in the night and then hides in his hole. But we will pass this test and with God's help we will survive and we will thrive."

GOD BLESS AMERICA!

That's our take. Yours in welcome.

December 2001
Our Opinion

Although the excitement of the war on terrorism is grabbing the headlines, we have looming on the horizon a stage play known as mid-term election in 2002. And, of course, we will begin to hear endless oratories about children without food, elders without medicine, and the demise of the Social Security system. One thing we probably won't hear is that our country has produced a society that offers unparalleled opportunity. Hopefully with the unity produced by the September 11th carnage, the language of class warfare will have no strategic traction. In acting as the protector of the bottom economic fifth of the population (income producers) politicians will begin to talk about the low income class in our country. These politicians, desiring nothing but power, assume that the same people show up in the bottom quintiles year after year, trapped in a rigid class society. In other words they assume zero income mobility.

"This is an old liberal trick "myth."

The Wall Street Journal recently reported the Federal Reserve Bank of Dallas in 1995 contained two surveys of income mobility. Over time most bottom quintiles moved up. The University of Michigan's panel survey on income dynamics tracked over three thousand people from 1975 to 1991. After seventeen years, only five percent of the bottom dwellers were still on the bottom. **That means that ninety-five percent moved up, over half made it to the middle-class quintiles and 29% were sitting plumply in the top fifth. Plus, the data suggests that once a person has reached the top, he or she has a good chance of remaining. Here's another interesting statistic: in 1975 the average gain in real income of those in the lower quartile was $25,322 by 1991. The people already in the top five percent in contrast were only $3,974 richer.**

The U. S. Treasury, which used different data in tracking 14,351 households from 1979 to 1988, found that eighty-six percent of those in the lowest income bracket moved up, 2/3 into the middle-class and almost fifteen percent into the top quartile.

So when the politicians begin spouting about the poor lower-class, have some sympathy, but by no means should you believe that everybody stays in that for the rest of their life. Education and a free market system can do wonders.

That's our take. Yours is welcome

Winter 2003
Our Opinion

"Don't tax thee. Don't tax me. Tax that man behind the tree."
One of our fingernail-on-the-blackboard moments is when the media uses the phrase, "cost of tax cuts." It is amazing to me that someone could consider that a tax cut would cost me something. If I am left with more money by virtue of a tax cut, why would that cost me something?

"Please don't forget…please, please read this paragraph again so you won't miss anything."

Oh, you say, 'It is not costing me; it is costing the federal government." Okay. As I see it then, if I get an increase in salary, I have more take home pay; that really doesn't cost me anything. The company I work for has probably cut some expenses so they can reward me with some of the benefits of, not only my work, but their profitability. Now that makes sense. Tax cuts do not cost the government money. If Washington doesn't get the money, it does not cost anything. Another thing that bothers us is when we hear that reducing the federal deficit during the prior administration's reign was responsible for the economic boom, making more capital available to business.

According to Holman Jenkins Jr. on the op-ed page of *The Wall Street Journal* late in 2002, "**No theory could be less comfortable in the company of the visible facts.** Both the Reagan boom and the current recovery plainly show that expanded deficits and declining interest rates can go hand in hand." Mr. Jenkins continues: "**A logical suspicion leaps to mind; interest rates are determined by inflation expectations, which in turn are shaped by confidence in monetary policy. The swinging of the federal budget from deficit to surplus and back again has little material impact on the cost of capital.**"

When will somebody recognize that a shortage of government revenues ("cost of a tax cut") is a function of inadequate growth rather that inadequate taxation.

When will somebody else figure out that there is more to it than dollars and cents?

Nobody can predict what a tax cut will do for the economy; nobody knows the complicated ways that government affects the willingness of individuals to earn, hire, and invest. It is no longer simply a matter of moving tax rates up and down in response to a rigid conception of the relationship between rates and revenues. Economists have been building up a picture of how tax law influences tax payer behavior in the real world since the Reagan tax cuts in the

'80s. Researchers have demonstrated the discouraging effect of high personal tax rates on investment and hiring by small entrepreneurs.

So when someone talks about "cost of a tax cut," it simply means that government will have to cut spending somewhere. And we would imagine there are a number of places where expenses could be cut that would not affect the everyday working taxpayer at all.

Growth is the answer. And the way we believe you generate growth is to look to the free market system by leaving more money in the public sector rather than increasing the growth of government.

THE WHOLE ELECTION PROCESS AND RESULTS IN THE FUTURE WILL REVOLVE AROUND TWO CENTERS: SHALL WE ACCEPT THE PHILOSOPHY OF RELYING ON THE GOVERNMENT TO EXPAND AND THUS INCREASE PROSPERITY OR SHALL WE ALLOW THE FREE MARKET SYSTEM TO GENERATE THE GROWTH THUS INCREASING THE REVENUE TO THE GOVERNMENT FOR USE IN A MEANINGFUL WAY TO "PROMOTE THE WELFARE OF THE PEOPLE?"

Only time will tell.

This is our take. Yours is welcome.

October 2003
Our Opinion

It has been our observation that during times of roaring bull markets, mutual funds always attract plenty of assets, especially those no-load funds which operate in aggressive arenas. Since performance drives most funds, attracting assets during those good times is not a difficult proposition. So the typical Bull Market investor says: 'If there's no sales charge, why should I pay one when I can get as great a return for free?' But then when things get tough and the markets turn down, or flatten, we find the old adage is still true—

"Mutual funds are not bought; they are distributed by real people." People begin to look to advisors for help.

It is quite difficult to buy or hold when markets are bearish without an advisor's encouragement.

During the times when nobody wants to buy, intelligent investors acquire shares at sometimes bargain prices, holding for the long-run. By having long-term-minded managers while reinvesting dividends at lower prices, the "buy and hold" investors own more shares than they started with as the market comes back.

"Let's roll the dice. I want 20% again!"

During treacherous markets, many investors have turned to Hedge Funds attempting to get the high double digit returns they enjoyed in the '90s.

Mr. Jack Bogle, with whom we agree in only a few cases, accurately points out in a recent issue of SunGard World that 700 Hedge Funds went out of business last year. That is almost one-sixth of them. Also for a Hedge Fund to deliver a 7% return after costs and taxes—and they are very tax efficient—they'll need to average about 15%, and that's not an extreme example.

If the stock market returns single-digit numbers over the next several years, it's easy to imagine the Hedge Fund managers taking quite a bit of risk to return to their shareholder 15%–20% after extremely high expenses.

With that knowledge, you can understand how Hedge Fund people at Canary Capital Partners would look for any advantage available.

We believe that all the mutual funds, investment company officials and unethical broker/dealers involved should be fined and, if illegal acts have occurred, be prosecuted to the fullest."

That's our take. Yours is welcome.

Occasionally, our local newspaper, *The Fort Worth Star Telegram*, uses articles from *The New York Times* or *The Washington Post* and other similar publications on their opinions and editorial page. We decided in this issue of *Opinions & Facts*, we would use one from *The Wall Street Journal*, which we solely agree with. We, of course, do not have their permission, so please, nobody call them and tell on us!!!

Riding the Omnibus

The Senate finally passed that $820 billion "omnibus" spending bill, and omnibus is certainly the word for it. According to an analysis by Taxpayers for Common Sense, this bill to finance much of the government for Fiscal Year 2004 contains an unprecedented 7,931 'earmarks' at a cost of $10.7 billion. Put another way, that's 15 sweetheart projects per Member.

There's $500,000 for a water taxi in Pittsburgh, $225,000 for the Wheels Museum in New Mexico, and $100,000 for "streetscaping" a tiny Salt Lake City neighborhood. In the cholesterol-subsidy category is $2 million to market specialty Wisconsin cheeses and goods. Alaska alone, home of Senate Appropriations Kingpin Ted Stevens, got 296 earmarked expenditures.

Among cutting-edge research grants are $450,000 to study "Sudden Oak Disease Syndrome" and $90,000 for an olive fruit fly study...in France. Some lucky folks at the University of Hawaii bagged $200,000 to produce "Primal Quest," a film about Kalahari Bushmen who pursue their prey until either man or animal drops from exhaustion. Which sounds a lot like the appropriations process.

Congress is now entering a brave new budget year, with President Bush promising to restrain spending, for a change. Word is that his budget proposal, due soon, will cap domestic non-defense discretionary spending growth at 1%, except for homeland security, which will grow by 10%. Congressional veterans know what that means: All of those earmarks will have to be stuffed into the homeland security basket.

Unless, of course, Mr. Bush breaks type and exercises his veto power. Failing that, we see that this year's omnibus bill contained $500,000 of the University of Akron to finance its "Exercise in Hard Choices" program—a simulation of the federal budget process. Maybe Congress should enroll.

(Someone told us there was also a sizeable grant to the National Cowgirl Museum here in Fort Worth. Please…say it's not true.)

That's our take. Yours is welcome.

Late Summer 2004
Our Opinion

Often we need to step back and take a look at the bigger picture rather than the short term view that most newspaper columnists, magazine writers, and politicians take. As our country moved into the industrial age, the agricultural industry lost many jobs. As we move into the technology world, from the industrial/manufacturing world, it will be necessary to have a newly trained workforce.

Make no mistake about it, if manufacturing jobs can be done overseas, at a lower cost than in this country, those jobs are going to move overseas. Whether we want to admit it or not, we are in a global economy.

"That's unpatriotic."

We saw that by imposing penalties on companies importing steel into our country during President Bush's first term, we have created threats by other countries which hurt the exporting of our manufactured goods overseas. As always, politicians look for the quick fix and short term result. Catering to the Union vote by closing our markets to low cost steel did not pay off.

Companies that deliver top-quality products and services will be the winners. It doesn't matter where they are based or where the work is done. That is the beauty of a free market system. It takes time to transition; if you don't believe it, just ask those guys who used to make buggy whips!

We are going through a long-range change in transitioning into a technological and information global society. It will not be painless; it will not be quickly accomplished; but it will vastly improve the world's standard of living."

That's our take... yours is welcome.

February 2001
Our Opinion

As the 21st century gets underway, we've learned the difference between production and consumption. The laws of economics have not been repealed. The weight in national and personal wealth is through production, and not consumption. Nations that produce more than they consume, tend to get wealthier. Making things takes capital, and capital itself takes many forms: It can be land, it can be labor, it can be money, or it can be capital goods (goods that create new value, new revenue, or new machines).

What we see in the market right now is a dispute between the "asset economy" and a "real economy." In an asset economy, you are encouraged to believe you can get rich by borrowing money to buy stocks and bonds and homes, which go up in value and pay for your retirement. In a real economy, economic growth and prosperity come from production, savings, and capital investment. Wise investors are not concerned about markets. They pay attention to individual companies which make up a market. These companies, in order to be successful, must compete globally. This takes leadership as well as capital.

The same truth applies to individuals. Our people must return to the job of reducing debt. When that happens, our savings will increase, and in this new era of an ownership society, we should come to a new time of prosperity.

Years of "easy, low-cost money" has not helped. But the pendulum has begun to swing. Let's hope we have the courage to return to fiscal sanity both as a nation and on an individual basis.

That's out take. Yours is welcome.

September 2003
Our Opinion

Notes from the Night….
09-10-03   Around the country, it appears that the State Attorneys General have been taking their own steps to put some allegedly crooked executives on the hot seat. The Oklahoma Attorney General has filed charges on Bernie Ebbers and it is difficult for us deal with the Federalies and go to a federal penitentiary instead of a state penitentiary. I understand the omelets are better there!

10-14-03   Meanwhile…At long last, many of the executives who've been charged with corporate crimes are now coming to trial. This is what always happens after market bubbles and lies have been told.

This is the way it is and the way that it should be. As we look to the future, let's hope that the people responsible for the looting of many corporations in this country will be not only be brought to trial, but prosecuted and given some prison time.

If you have read the newspapers and you've seen our latest *Special Edition – Opinions & Facts*, you've noted that quite a number of mutual fund executives have turned out to be as greedy and unethical as many of their friends who managed the company in which the funds buy stock. That too, will come to an end and we will all discover that the fund companies that have cared more about their customer's long-term approach to investing than they do hedge-fund managers who have attempted to line their own pockets by taking advantage of the everyday long-term investor, will also be put into the proper surroundings.

"You can bet on this—no problem."

We are convinced that the fund groups **and brokerage firms** who think about their shareholders, charging low and reasonable fees, and giving good service rather than seeking simply to collect assets, will profit and benefit in the future.

11-05-03   The shoes continue to drop. The Putnam Funds have come under fire by the regulators and are being called to task for their mutual fund managers' alleged market timing. We've said many times that market timing does not work (unless of course you buy and sell after the market closes!)

It appears that Eliot Spitzer, the Attorney General of New York, is being successful in encouraging the SEC and the industry to come up with some sort of regulatory controls to stop this unethical activity. Of course as always happens, when the regulators get into it, they will over regulate, and since mutual fund investors are also voters, Congress has gotten their hands in it too.

As we told you in our last *Opinions & Facts*, people who manage the funds we're most concerned about are on the cutting edge of honesty and ethical conduct. This pleases us to no end, and we will continue to honor those long term relationships we have with the quality money managers to whom you've trusted your funds.

And the beat goes on…

12-03-03   As far as the recent investigations by the Securities and Exchange Commission and the New York State Attorney General, new allegations have come forth. The Invesco Group, The Strong Group of funds and The Pilgrim Baxter Group have all been accused of various crimes and some of the officials have been charged with fraud. There are a number of funds under investigation; incidentally, we've noticed that the outstanding names that have come to the surface have all been, from a retail standpoint, no-load funds. With the exception of Putnam, all the funds have smaller asset bases and as we see now, they're being reduced quite rapidly.

If there was ever a time that the public should consider checking out the reliability and integrity of their advisor, it is now. If you recall, as I do, that very seldom does a news paper or magazine columnist recommend to his readers that they should consider using an advisor and suggest a commission or a fee. Remember, the columnist is not under scrutiny from the SEC or The National Association of Security Dealers. Since the first amendment holds true for financial columnists as well as others in the media, they can write pretty much what they want to write, make pretty much any recommendations they want to make, and have very few problems in facing any fiduciary responsibilities.

Recently, a column in a local newspaper pointed out several things that you should ask any person giving you advice on investing. We hope to run those in our next end of the year newsletter.

At any rate, we would certainly hope before this so called scandal is over, that the large Wall Street firms will answer to the public about taking special fees from the funds for "shelf space" and paying their brokers more to sell these funds rather than others which might fit the situation better.

Always feel free to call us with questions. We have made an attempt to always give you full disclosure in regards to our firm.

That's out take. Yours is welcome.

January 2013
Our Opinion

While we have purposely established this Opinion section with no particular timeline, I'd like to end it with some pertinent quotes from a *Wall Street Journal* column by Sohrab Ahmari, who is an assistant books editor at the Journal. The information comes from an interview with Mr. Harvey Mansfield an eminent political scientist who's been a professor at Harvard for the last 50 years. Mr. Mansfield is 80 years old; he was a Fullbright scholar in London and spent a 2 year stint in the Army. After the war he returned to Harvard for a Doctorate and it was then that Mr. Mansfield said, "My initiating forces were anticommunism and my perception at Democrats were solved on Communism, to use a rather unpleasant phrase from the time—unpleasant but true." This December 1–3, 2012 Opinions column of *The Wall Street Journal* reveals some intriguing and distinctive ideas on Democracy. While all readers will not agree with this 2013 final "Opinion"—Neither will they necessarily agree with our approach to investing philosophy. So be it. We love the First Amendment!

In his interview with Mr. Ahmari, Mr. Mansfield says, consider voting: *"You can count voters and votes, and political science does that a lot and that's very useful because votes are in fact countable. One counts for one. But if we get serious about what it means to vote, we immediately go to the notion of an informed voter. AND IF YOU GET SERIOUS ABOUT THAT, YOU GO ALL THE WAY TO VOTING AS A WISE CHOICE. THAT WOULD BE A TRUE VOTER. THE OTHERS ARE ALL LESSER VOTERS OR EVEN NOT VOTING AT ALL." MR. MANSFIELD CONTINUES; "THEY'RE JUST INDICATING A BELIEF, OR WHIM, BUT NOT MAKING A WISE CHOICE. THAT'S PROBABLY BECAUSE THEY'RE NOT WISE."*

This is a straight quote from Mr. Mansfield:

> *"By that measure, the electrets that granted Barack Obama a second term were unwise—the President achieved a victory." Mr. Mansfield says, "The Democrats said nothing about their plans for the future. All they did was attack the other side. Obama's campaign consisted entirely of saying 'I'm on your side' to the American people, to those in the middle. No matter what comes next, this silence about the future is ominous."*

Mr. Mansfield addresses The Progressive Movement: He says; that movement depends on the idea that things will get better and progress will be made in the actualization of equality." He points out that the 2012 campaign Progressives were "confined" to defining what they've already achieved or making small improvements – student loans, free condoms, etc.

In an interesting statement Mr. Mansfield says, *"Democrats refusal to address the future in positive terms also reveals the parties intent to create an entitlement or welfare state that takes issues off the bargaining table and renders them above politics."* The end goal, Mr. Mansfield worries, is to sideline the American Constitutional tradition in favor of a practical Constitution consisting of progressive measures the Left has passed that cannot be revoked and that is what would be fixed in our political system, not the Constitution. "Social scientists and political scientists are very much involved in the foundation of the progressive movement. What these experts did was find ways to improve the wellbeing of the poor, the incompetent, all those who have the right to vote but can't quite govern their own lives. And still to this day we see in the Democratic Party the alliance between the PHDs and the victims."

Mr. Mansfield points out that within Democracy "there is good and bad, free and slave," and that "Democracy can produce a slavish mind and a slavish country." The political task before every generation, Mr. Mansfield understands, is to "defend the good kind of Democracy and to do what you have to be aware of human *differences and inequalities, especially intellectual inequalities.* Progressives take things further. They think that the main use of liberty is to create more equality. They don't see that there is such a thing as too much equality and they don't see limits to Democratic equalizing. They can't understand how wealth redistribution can not only bankrupt the public, but corrupt the national soul. "He says the American people frequently "protect inequalities by voting not to destroy or deprive the rich of their riches. They don't vote for all the measures of equalization, for which they get condemned as suffering from false consciousness. But that's true consciousness because the American people want to make Democracy work and so do the Conservatives. Liberals on the other hand just want to make Democracy more Democratic."

Mr. Mansfield goes on to say that equality untendered by liberty invites disaster. There is a difference between making a form of government more like itself and making it viable. He goes deeper by saying, "While Entitlements are an attack on the common good, they signal a warning sign and seem in good stead. That is until the government goes broke, as has occurred across Europe. The problems that we run into are that we don't count the cost when we look at the things we desire."

Mr. Mansfield goes on to point out that American elites today prefer to dismiss the "unchangeable, undemocratic facts" about human inequality. **Progressives go further: "They think that the main use of liberty is to create more equality.** They don't see that there is such a thing as too much equality. They don't see limits to Democratic equalizing how, say, wealth distribution will not only bankrupt the public fiscal but corrupt the national soul." Americans, Mr. Mansfield says take inequality for granted. "**The American people frequently protect inequalities by voting not to destroy or deprive the rich of their riches.** They don't vote for all measures of equalization for which they get condemned as suffering from false consciousness. Liberals on the other hand just want to make Democracy more Democratic." Mr. Mansfield continues, "**Equality untempered by liberty invites disaster. Pushed to its extremes, Democracy can lead to 'mass rule by an ignorant or uncaring government'.**" This takes us to the concept of entitlements and what are they? In our judgment they are an attack on the human good. As Mr. Mansfield says, "Entitlements say that I get mine no matter what the state of the country is when I get it. So it's like a bond or an annuity. What the entitlement does is give the government a version of a private security which is better because the government provides a better guarantee than a private company can." Mr. Mansfield continues, "Cost is just an economic word for the common good. In fact, we cannot afford entitlements as they are since we've always underestimated the cost." Mr. Mansfield points out that principals are necessary for the common good. They need to be there so that judgment can be distinguished from opportunism. But just because you give ground on principal doesn't mean that you're an opportunist.

> *This leads us to comment that it's important that our educational system teach the poor and vulnerable to become a little more independent and to prize independence and not just live for a government check.*

And interestingly enough Mr. Mansfield says, "Self government is within each self, and where are you going to get that except with morality, responsibility and religion.

And when you look at the problems that we face in this country, maybe the needs for better and stronger educational methods are the most important goal that our common good could hope for. After all, what good is a vote if that vote is one that carries with it intellectual blindness.

That's our take. Yours is welcome

www.ingramcontent.com/pod-product-compliance
Lightning Source LLC
Chambersburg PA
CBHW060609200326
41521CB00007B/707